RED SEA

Shlomo Cohen

SEAPEN BOOKS

SEAPEN BOOKS
42 Gordon St. Tel Aviv 63414 Israel.
Telex: 341343 ET IN.

All maps based upon geographic survey of "Survey of Israel", Ministry of Labor, State of Israel, except for those produced by POINTOUT PRODUCTIONS LTD. on pages 34-37.

1st Impression 1975.
2nd Impression 1988, only partly revised due to political changes in the area.

Printed in Israel at the Chavatzelet Press, Herzlia.

ISBN: 965-362-000-2

RED SEA SPORTS CLUB

A Right Royal Sports Club

ANDROMEDA
Cruise along the coastline – excursions to Taba Beach daily.

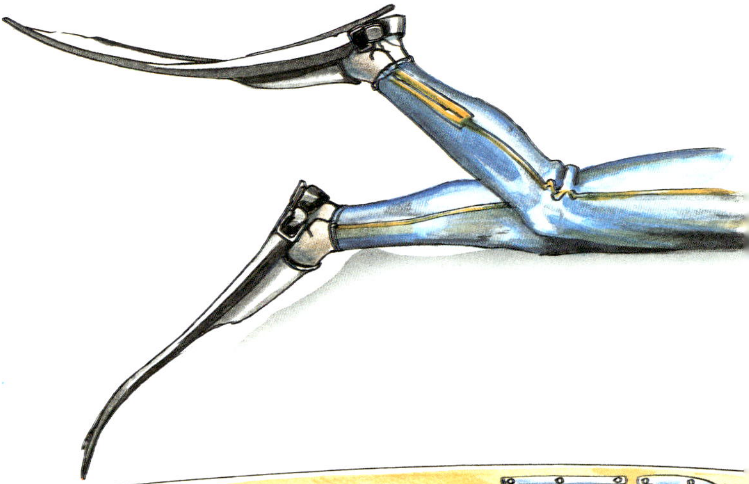

FLOTILLA
Fun for the whole family! Sailing daily in the Bay of Eilat.

MOTORBOAT RENTAL
Drive yourself!

SAILBOATS
Kayaks and paddleboats.

WATERSKIING
For beginners and advanced skiers alike! Daily 9:00-18.00.

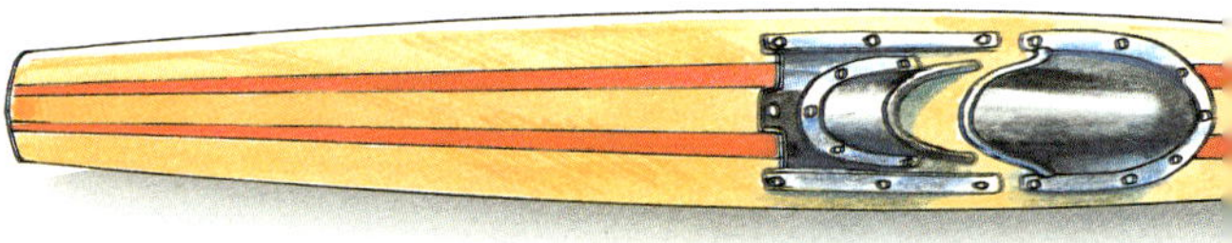

DEEP-SEA FISHING
Go for the big ones – tuna, barracuda and other game fish!

SAFARI
Make tracks – take a jeep on a desert adventure!

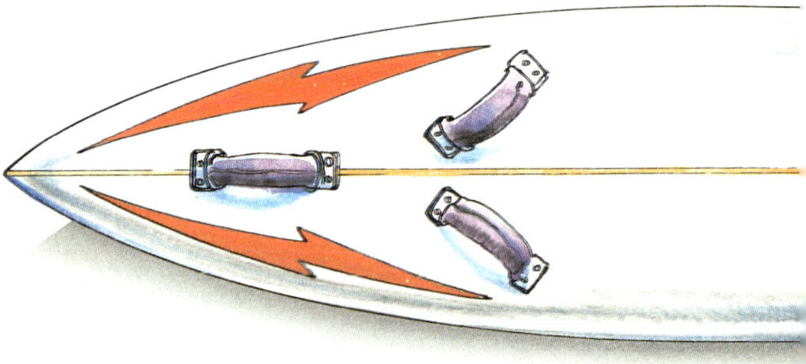

BICYCLE RENTAL
Pedal-power...ride around Eilat!

BIRD WATCHING

RED SEA SPORTS FASHION WEAR

WINDSURFING COURSES & RENTAL
Try your hand at windsurfing at any of three select locations – The Lagoon, North Beach and Coral Beach.

SCUBA DIVING & COURSES
For all levels and all ages, under the guidance of our professional instructors. See the splendor of the famous Coral Gardens of Eilat! Diving at King Solomon's Palace and the Caravan Hotel.

TEXAS RANCH
Horseback riding – expert tuition available.

RED SEA SPORTS CLUB
King Solomon's Wharf, North Beach Eilat 88000, Israel.
Tel: (059) 79685, 79111, 76569, 73725. Telex: 7753,7751 RSSC IL

The Red Sea Diver's Guide
Written, designed and illustrated by ***Shlomo Cohen***

Contributors
Fish Index ***David Fridman***
Diving ***Willy Halpert***
Medicine ***Dr. Yehuda Melamed***
Photography ***David Doubilet***
Windsurfing ***Andy Uselius***
English translation ***Shlomo Cohen with Frank Jones***
Design Assistant ***Roni Kallner-Cohen***
Text Editor ***Louise Shabat-Bethlehem***

With gratitude to ***Michael Daniel*** *and* ***Eliezer Taragan,***
who initiated the first publication.

Dedicated to the memory of Dan Nacht

Photographs by

Alex Arbell:	83, 88b, 107T, 114T, 118B, 119B, 122B, 128B, 129, 130T, 134T, 135TL, 142B.
Werner Braun:	103C, 104, 110T, 111B, 117B, 123B, 124, 127B, 130B, 144.
Shlomo Cohen:	38B, 39, 42B, 43, 44, 47, 48, 52, 54, 56, 58, 62, 64, 66, 69, 70, 73, 74, 76, 77, 78, 80, 88T, 92, 93, 94, 99, 100T, 102T, 105, 106T, 111T, 112T, 113C, 114B, 118T, 121, 122T, 123C, 125B, 131, 132, 133B, 135TR&B, 143, 145.
Yoske Galili:	65.
Itamar Grinberg:	38T, 42T, 46
Maty Grünberg:	72, 82, 84.
Willy Halpert:	45, 108, 115T.
Michael Hoff:	49, 53, 55, 57, 59, 63, 67, 71, 75, 79, 81, 89, 91, 95.
Dan Nacht:	17, 61, 68.
David Pilosof:	113T&B.
Howard Rosenstein:	19, 50, 51, 87, 103B, 109T, 110B, 112B, 115C&B, 116T, 125T, 127T, 136, 137, 140, 141, 152.
Yaacov Yitzhak:	100B, 101B, 102B, 103T, 106B, 107B, 109B, 116B, 117T, 119T, 120T, 123T, 126, 128T, 134B.

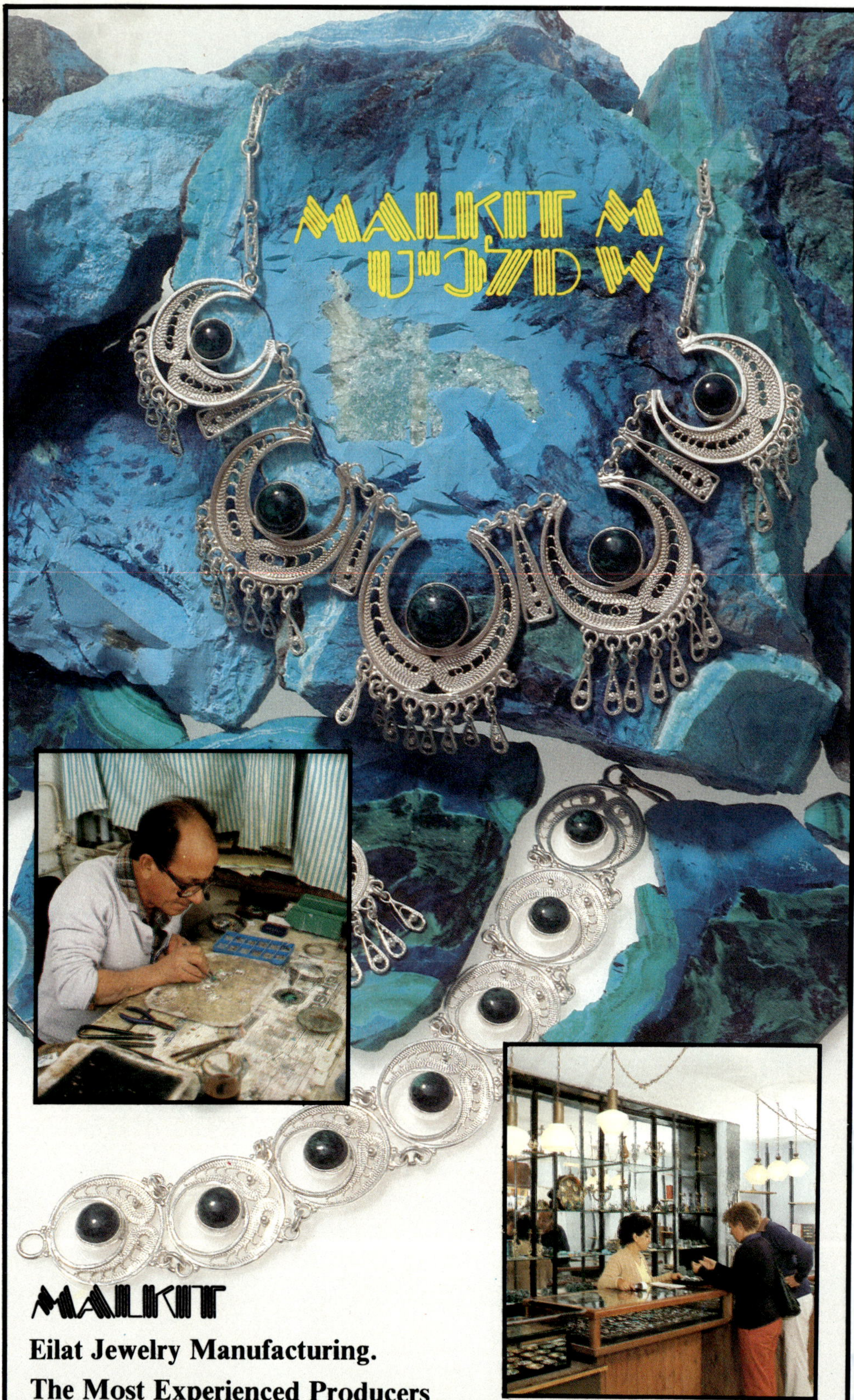

MALKIT

Eilat Jewelry Manufacturing.

The Most Experienced Producers of Eilat Stone!

A family concern with a legacy of tradition and fine craftsmanship, MALKIT was the first to exploit the unique Eilat stone in its designs. Our original creations in gold, silver and Eilat stone may be purchased in our showroom. Alternatively, jewelry may be ordered to your own personal specifications.

The MALKIT Exhibition is open weekdays 08:00 - 19:00. Fridays, Saturdays and holidays 08:00 - 13:00. Tel: (059) 73372, 75650.457 Schunat Hadekel P.O. Box 1253 Eilat.

CONTENTS

WHY THE RED SEA?

And King Solomon made a navy of ships in Etzion-geber, which is beside Eloth, on the shore of the Red Sea, in the land of Edom. And Hiram sent in the navy his servants, shipmen that had knowledge of the sea, with the servants of Solomon. And they came to Ophir, and fetched from thence gold, four hundred and twenty talents, and brought it to King Solomon.

I Kings, 9

If King Solomon had felt the whim to leave Jerusalem and cross the barren Negev Desert to Eloth – modern "Eilat" today – and if he had plunged his royal visage into the clear water of the Red Sea, well, it's a bit doubtful whether his import-export business in spices, peacocks, apes and gold would have shown much profit.

And if the sagacious king had lounged on the warm sands at the Gulf of Eilat, watching an ochre sun disappear gently behind the incredible mountains of Sinai, perhaps a throne would have been left empty in Jerusalem and his *SONG OF SONGS* would have gained a different, even more exotic character. No doubt King Solomon would have ordered a biblical version of our modern diving mask, and would have busily explored the magnificent corals. He wouldn't have bothered to take his head out of the water even if the Queen of Sheba herself was standing behind him.

But then, King Solomon didn't leave his throne for the crystal waters of that gulf, and he holds us not in his debt for another epic poem about the "good life" around its shores. The citizenry of Sodom, on the other hand, brought an ill wind from the Lord's displeasure, that gave us some good: a tectonic earthquake which destroyed their town and neighbouring Gomorrah, created the Gulf of Eilat.

The Gulf of Eilat defines the eastern shore of the Sinai Peninsula: where Asia and Africa meet. This great land bridge connecting two great continents has remained the stage where nations and major civilizations have met, mingled and warred from the beginning of history to the present day. And yet, by some remarkable paradox of history, it remains one of the few places on earth almost completely untouched by modern civilization.

The marginal tropical waters sustain an overwhelming variety of marine flora and fauna, with more than 1000 species of fish feeding among spectacular coral. The intensity and colour of their world is magnified by the stark terrestrial contrast of an arid desert landscape, stretching in pastel colours as far as the eye can reach. Lawrence of Arabia described the desolate moon valleys and peaks of Sinai: "In the hillsides all sorts of rocks are mingled in confusion; grey-green limestone cliffs run down sheer for hundreds of feet, in tremendous ravines whose faces are a medley of colours wherever crags of black porphyry and diorite jut out, or wherever soft sandstone, washed down, has left long pink and white smudges on the lighter colours."

Just a few steps away, a diving mask opens another dimension of existence in tropical colour and pulsating rhythms of life.

We call it the "Gulf of Eilat". It appears as "Gulf of Akaba" on the classic British Admiralty maps. Biblical narrative refers to the "Sea of Reeds" or the "Red Sea". Regardless of your choice, when a perfect calm meets the setting sun, its light reflected from the red Mountains of Edom and Median in Jordan and Saudia, the deep steel-blue water turns a crimson shade, making it indeed a red sea.

Shlomo Cohen.

INTRODUCTION

Where Is it?

The Red Sea is a branch of the Indian Ocean beginning at the Straits of Bab Al Mandab, between Yemen and Ethiopia, and then climbing north-west to 27°43'N where the Sinai Peninsula divides it into two long narrow gulfs: Eilat and Suez.

Sinai itself reaches a length of about 400 km. (250 mi.) and a width of about 250 km. (155 mi.) with an area of 61,000 sq.km. (23,000sq.mi.). The peninsula is easily divided into two major topographic zones. In the north one finds a desert plain and to the south a mountainous region representing the continuation of a great mountain range reaching from deep in Saudia Arabia across Sinai and thence to Nubia on the African continent.

The Gulf of Eilat belongs to southern Sinai and, therefore, it places your diving sites next to some of the most barren, intriguing and breathtaking mountain landscapes in the world. Southern Sinai separates itself into four basic topographic sub-divisions: 1) a plain of sand and rock stretching east from the northern tip of the Gulf of Suez to the northern end of the Gulf of Eilat; 2) the alluvial plain along the western shore beginning at the northern tip of the Gulf of Suez and ending at Ras Muhammed; 3) the central massif reaching an altitude of 2,642 m. (8,718.6 ft.); 4) the eastern shore of beaches and fringing reef, interrupted intermittently by mountains and alluvial fans, from Eilat to Ras Nasrani.

Geologists assert that Sinai is still drifting east from Africa, where it was once joined, thus still enlarging the Gulf of Suez on its western shore. The Gulf of Eilat on the eastern shore of Sinai was created, however, by the Syrian-East African Rift. As the land bridge connecting Asia and Africa, Sinai has been of immense historical, economic, political and cultural significance throughout the pages of history.

A Flow of History

During the early Biblical period Sinai represented little more than a barren wilderness separating Canaan from Egypt. Later, however, the Egyptian dynasties used this desert as a springboard into the Land of Israel and Syria. As has been mentioned, Solomon, the son of King David, built his port of Etzion Geber near Eloth during the epoch of the Israelite kingdoms and established a thriving trade with the mysterious Ophir (perhaps Yemen) and possibly India.

In ancient days the Red Sea and its two gulfs were used as major trade routes periodically. During the Graeco-Roman period a thriving trade from India and the Middle East developed with the nations of the Mediterranean basin utilizing the Red Sea as the swiftest and safest passage. This inaugurated a stiff competition for maritime traffic between the two gulfs still continuing in some measure till today. The city of Suez in that age was a Greek port known as "Annapolis". After their conquest of Egypt the Persians tried to further the development of this trade center by digging a canal from the Nile River to the Gulf of Suez. (Not an original concept as the Pharaohs had built such a canal.) However as their Egyptian subjects began to throw off the yoke of domination, the Persians also developed Eilat in cooperation with the Nabateans to provide alternative overland passage to the Red Sea.

Following the conquests of Alexander the Great and the succeeding dynasties of the Ptolemies, the Nabateans feared that Suez would, once again, gain predominance as the trading center to the East. So they nurtured the route from the Gulf of Eilat to Gaza, which then grew to the status of a major port for the Mediterranean trade. During the reign of Ptolemy II, Egypt gained control of all trade routes on the Red Sea. Eilat was conquered along with almost the entire eastern shore of the Red Sea to the southern tip of Arabia. Having lost all their ports, the Nabateans were forced to develop caravan routes east to the Persian Gulf. With the bitter Seleucid Wars among the heirs of Alexander, all trade with India diminished and along with it the importance of the Red Sea for international commerce.

Its importance revived again when the Egyptians succeeded in navigating the southern tip of Aden to reach India. They reopened the trade route to Suez and thence to Alexandria and Rome, bypassing Eilat.

The Roman Empire gained control of the Red Sea when Augustus Caesar defeated the Ptolemies and placed Roman garrisons as far south as Aden. Trade with India accelerated with most merchandise passing through Suez. The Nabateans were reduced to the status of an agricultural society. As the economy of Egypt declined, followed by the usual unrest, the Romans occupied Eilat with the Tenth Roman Legion and developed the region.

The Gulf of Eilat reached its zenith, however, during the Byzantine Period. Egypt would not grant passage through its territories to the Byzantine Empire and so it utilized the Eilat trade route. The Monastery of Santa Katerina was founded during this period, emphasizing the area's religious significance to Judeo-Christian history.

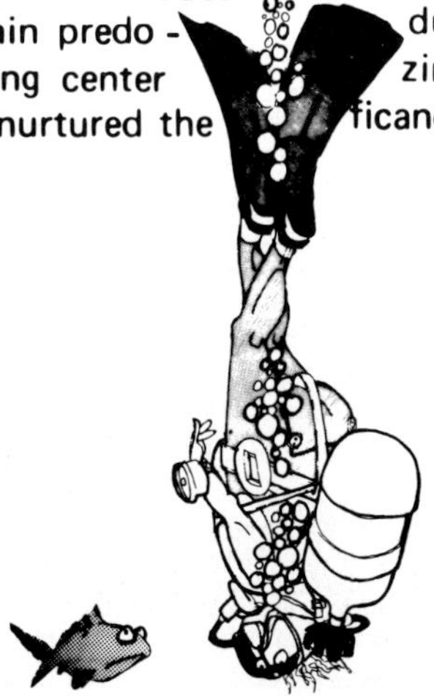

Following the Moslem conquests of Israel and North Africa in the 7th century, the importance of this area for maritime trade once again declined. Sinai became a pilgrimage route to Medina and Mecca but the Moslem masses preferred land passage to their holy cities rather than a sea voyage.

During the Crusader conquests, the Christian knights controlled these pilgrimage routes across northern Sinai. The Moslem ruler of Egypt, Saladin, bypassed northern Sinai by conquering Eilat and opening an alternate way to Mecca from its gulf. This conquest forced the Crusaders to abandon their strategy of controlling the pilgrimages by holding the peninsula's northern desert and they determined to take Eilat. Reynaud de Chatillon led a Crusader force to Eilat from Gaza in 1183, carrying prefabricated ships on camelback across the Negev Desert, and wrested control of the eastern gulf from Saladin. Chatillon began raiding the coast of Arabia and became a serious threat to Mecca itself. This aroused the entire Moslem world. Not only was their holy city threatened but the lucrative trade routes to India. In alliance with the Caliph of Damascus, heretofore unattainable, Saladin defeated the Crusader armies at the Horns of Hittin near the Sea of Galilee and entered Jerusalem, eliminating Crusader influence in the south and pushing them back to the ports on the coastal plain of the Mediterranean.

At the close of the Crusader Era, Sinai again became an important sea route to Mecca, Medina and India via the Red Sea. Until the beginning of the 16th century, first under the Mamelukes and then in the Ottoman Empire, peace and relative tranquility reigned supreme in the gulfs. But in this century trade competition developed between Portugal and the Ottoman Empire. Portuguese navigators explored and mapped a sea voyage to India around the southern tip of Africa. They attacked and defeated Ottoman strongholds both at the Straits of Bab Al Mandab and the Persian Gulf, putting an end to the Red Sea as a major trade channel until the end of the 19th century. The coffee trade, however, from Mocha and Yemen continued from ports in the Gulf of Eilat.

British interest in the region developed at the beginning of the 19th century. Upon their completion of the Suez Canal in 1869 (with major financial support from the English branch of the Rothschilds), and the development of steam ships, Europe led by England, gained control of trade with East Africa, India and the Persian Gulf. Once again, of course, the Gulf of Eilat lost its importance.

The Ottoman Empire revived interest in the area before World War I, with support from Germany, and began the Hejaz Railroad from Amman to the port of Akaba, intended to open a new pilgrimage road to Mecca and provide an alternative trade passage to India uncontrolled by England. This prompted the British to send warships up the Gulf of Eilat. They threatened war with Turkey and forced the Ottoman Empire to cede the greater portion of Sinai, along a western line, from El Arish to Taba Bay, to England under the administration of the British Governor in Cairo. Thus ended several centuries of Turkish rule over the peninsula.

World attention again focused on the Gulf of Eilat during World War II when Rommel's "desert rats" of the Afrika Korps almost reached the Suez Canal. Allied strategists seriously considered using the Gulf of Eilat as a logistical alternative to the Far East.

In 1948 with U.N. recognition of the reborn modern State of Israel the Gulf of Eilat became important both to the Kingdom of Jordan, with its port of Akaba, and Israel, with its modern version of Solomon's Biblical Eloth. Both Israel's Sinai Campaign and Six Day War were fought over Egyptian closure of the Straits of Tiran — key for exports to Africa, Australia and the Far East, and for the import of vital oil from the Persian Gulf.

The Gulf of Eilat

The two gulfs divided by the Sinai Peninsula are markedly different. Suez is long and wide and relatively shallow with a maximum depth of 85 m. (280.5 ft.). Eilat is much narrower and deeper, being a part of the great Syrian-East African Rift (Fig. 1). It extends for 180 km. (113.4 mi.) from the Straits of Tiran to the port of Eilat. At its northernmost point it is 5 km. (3.2 mi.) wide and reaches a maximum width of 28 km. (18 mi.) opposite Dahab. (For diving ease this edition includes the coast of Ras Muhammed although it is not within the Gulf of Eilat.)

Perusing a bathymetric map (Fig. 2) you will note how the Gulf of Eilat bottoms in the form of a v-shaped trench and, therefore one may sound great depths a short distance from shore. Two major marine basins create and are responsible for its great depth. The northern basin extends south to Nuweiba and reaches a maximum depth of 1,000 m. (3,300 ft.) while the southern valley extends to the Straits of Tiran and sounds at 1,800 m. (5,940 ft.) opposite El Hibek.

1

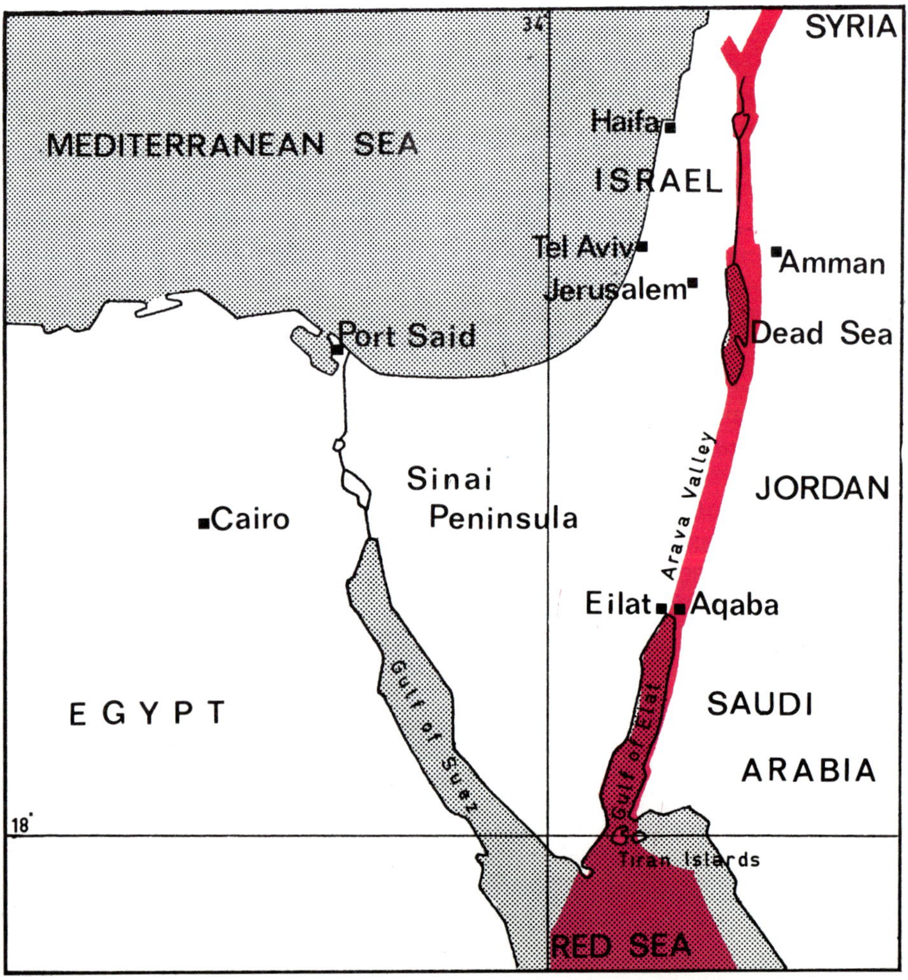

2

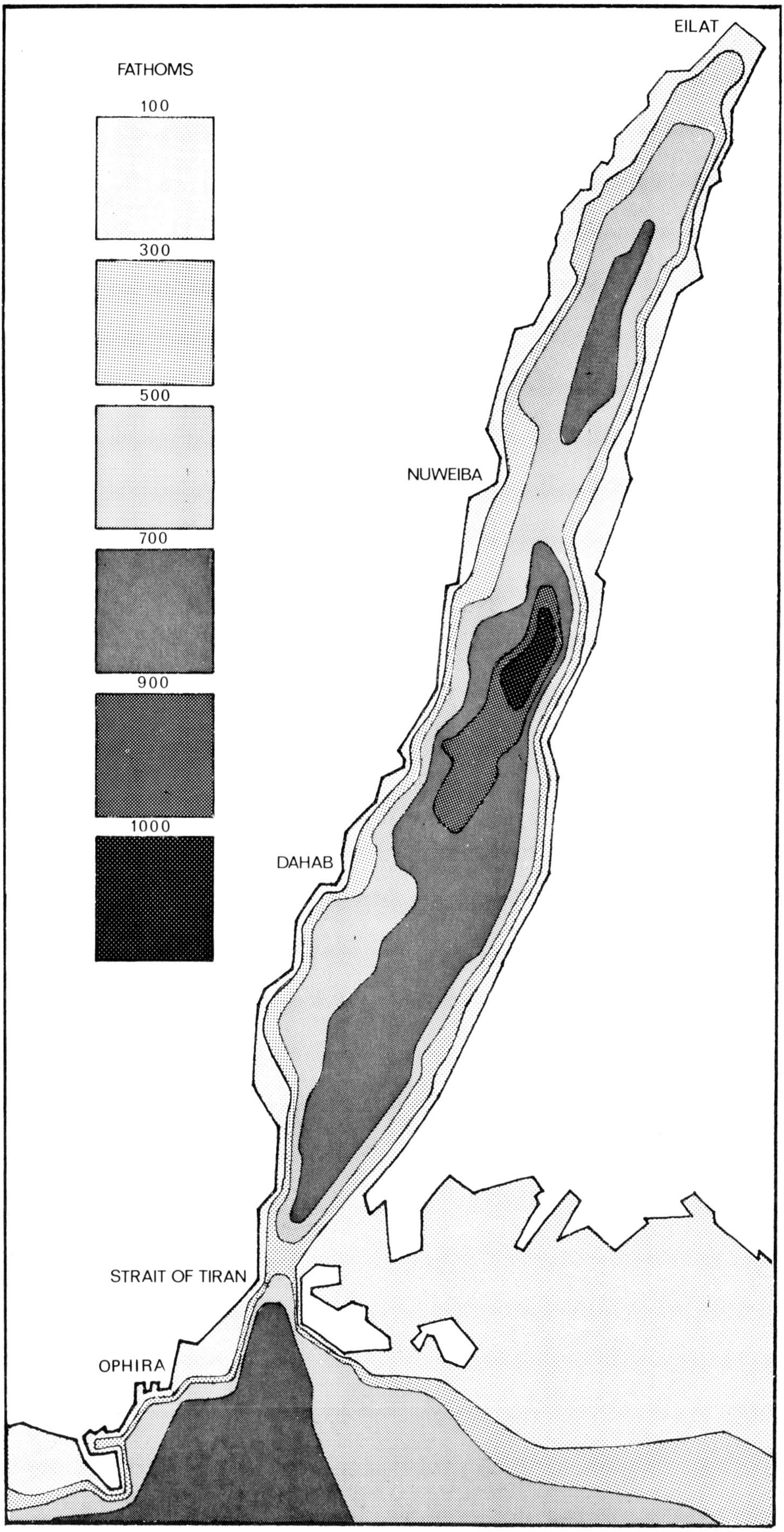
FATHOMS
100
300
500
700
900
1000
EILAT
NUWEIBA
DAHAB
STRAIT OF TIRAN
OPHIRA

The Islands of Tiran and Snapir (belonging to Saudia Arabia) block the entrance to the Gulf. A chain of reefs connect them with Arabia in the east and Sinai in the west. The Tiran Straits are between that island of the same name and Sinai, about 6 km. (4 mi.) wide, and occupied by four huge reef patches that have claimed many ships through the centuries. Most captains even today still plot their voyage to provide daylight navigation through this entrance. These four reef patches – Gordon, Thomas, Woodhouse, and Jackson – are separated by deep rifts between 40–80 m. (132 – 264 ft.) deep. The tides create strong currents between these reefs.

Only two channels are considered safe for marine navigation: 1) "Enterprise Passage" between Gordon Reef and the Sinai shore with a width of 1,200 m. (3,960 ft.) and a depth of 300 m. (990 ft.), and 2) "Grafton Channel" between Jackson Reef and the Island of Tiran with a width of 800 m. (2,640 ft.) and a depth of 70 m. (231 ft). Sounding east from Tiran and Snapir to Saudia Arabia one finds maximum depths of 10 m. (33 ft.).

The western shore of the Gulf of Eilat and the Sinai coast to Ras Muhammed, described in this volume, possesses three distinct morphological characteristics. From Eilat to Ras A-Tantur one finds a long and narrow shore – almost the entire length of the Gulf. It is a product of the great Rift creating high mountains descending steeply into the sea, later filled by numerous alluvial fans. Because of this steep v-shaped trench only two large drainage systems succeeded in creating major deltas at Nuweiba and Dahab. Not only is the shore interrupted by fans but one also finds locations without beach where the mountains march straight into the sea, such as at Nakab Shaheen. Only one significant bay may be found along this entire stretch of coast: the Fijord. The remainder are minor breaks between fans.

The second morphological zone reaches from Ras A-Tantur to Ras Nasrani. It is similar to the first zone but much wider, generally 5 km. (3 mi.) from mountains to the sea. This entire area was created by the drainage from Wadis Kid and Um Adoui, leaving a gentle slope composed of alluvial debris. The stands of mangrove at Nabek are this shoreline's most prominent feature.

From Ras Nasrani at the Straits of Tiran to Ras Muhammed one discovers the third zone where the coastline gradually alters as the beaches are progressively replaced by bluffs of fossil coral lifted up from the ocean floor.

Weather

The Sinai Peninsula belongs to that arid desert belt encircling the globe in the Northern Hemisphere. Sinai may be divided into three climate zones following a morphological pattern: the east coast of the Gulf of Suez, the mountains of southern Sinai, and the west coast of the Gulf of Eilat. The weather systems responsible for winter rains in the eastern Mediterranean generally do not reach further south than 31°N. Only when such a system dips below that latitude may rains reach the peninsula. Such low pressure systems from the Mediterranean are principally responsible for both precipitation and sand storms over Sinai. During the change of seasons, however, low pressure systems developing in the Sahara draw hot, dry desert East winds from Asia minor causing dramatic rises in temperature often accompanied by sand storms. The change of seasons may also see lows developing over the Red Sea, bringing moist tropical air from the south and creating cloud cover, haze, electrical storms and just occasionally – rain.

The western shore of the Gulf is influenced by the topography of the Syrian-East African Rift, the ocean itself, and the Sinai mountains. This area, being a narrow coastal strip, experiences changes in weather from north to south due to the prevailing north winds that bring dry desert air becoming progressively more moisture laden as it descends the Gulf. The prevailing northerlies funneled to the Gulf by the Rift's Arava Valley are only slightly influenced by offshore winds: in an easterly direction during the day and westerly at night.

As one descends south along the Gulf the open sea exerts an increasingly profound influence upon the prevailing north winds. The famous and rare "south storms", always in the summer, can reach a maximum velocity of between 8 and 9 on the Beaufort Scale (See Appendix No. 1).

The land mass in the north is the primary influence over temperatures in the Gulf but this diminishes to the south as one approaches open sea. Because of the moderating effect of the open sea an interesting temperature pattern appears: maximum temperatures in the summer are lower in the south while minimum temperatures are higher in the north and this reverses during the winter when maximums are higher in the south and minimums lower in the north. (See Appendix No. 3).

The coldest month of the year is January and the hottest are July and August.

Water temperatures of the Gulf are higher in the north. The lowest water temperatures occur in February with the highs in August and September. Year around they range between 21–26°C. without being effected by daily atmospheric temperatures or passing weather systems.

The Gulf of Eilat is an unusually quiet body of water. Wave action from the prevailing northerlies gradually builds up from Eilat to reach its peak at Dahab where it diminishes again to the Straits of Tiran. Waves at Eilat can reach a maximum of 3.5 m. (11.6 ft.) during the rare "south storms". Ras Muhammed is more sheltered from the prevailing north winds and influenced primarily by southerlies from the sea and local wind conditions, permitting maximum crests of 4.5 m (15 ft.). Compared to their local diving conditions most visiting divers find the Gulf waters a "paradise" with clear visibility, little wave action, almost no current, and warm temperatures the year around.

The Coral Reef

Two elements characteristic of tropical waters are found in your diving area: coral reef and mangroves. The word "mangrove" is a general name for those bushes and trees growing in mud or shallow water, anchored to the bottom but with their roots exposed to the air. The most common species found in this region is *Aviccenia marina* reaching a maximum **highth** of 3–4 m. (10–13 ft.) in sufficient water or appearing as low bushes in sandy soil.

The coral reefs are created by polyp colonies building exoskeletons of calcium carbonate. For great geologic periods their calcium waste has been deposited by countless generations to build a solid block of reef, covered by a thin veil of living polyps continuing the process. Coral may develop from sea-level to 100 m. (330 ft.) depths although their population density diminishes progressively at greater depths and their shapes also undergo change.

Two ecological prerequisites are necessary for coral development: 1) clear water is absolutely necessary as sediments kill polyps and 2) a steady current to bring food, permit healthy respiration and to carry off waste.

Corals in the Gulf of Eilat build fringing reefs developing off-shore and usually creating a table. The direction of a reef is determined by the direction of the current and its strength. The schematic drawing that follows provides a clear understanding of reef terminology with reference to their various topographic features typical of coral development.

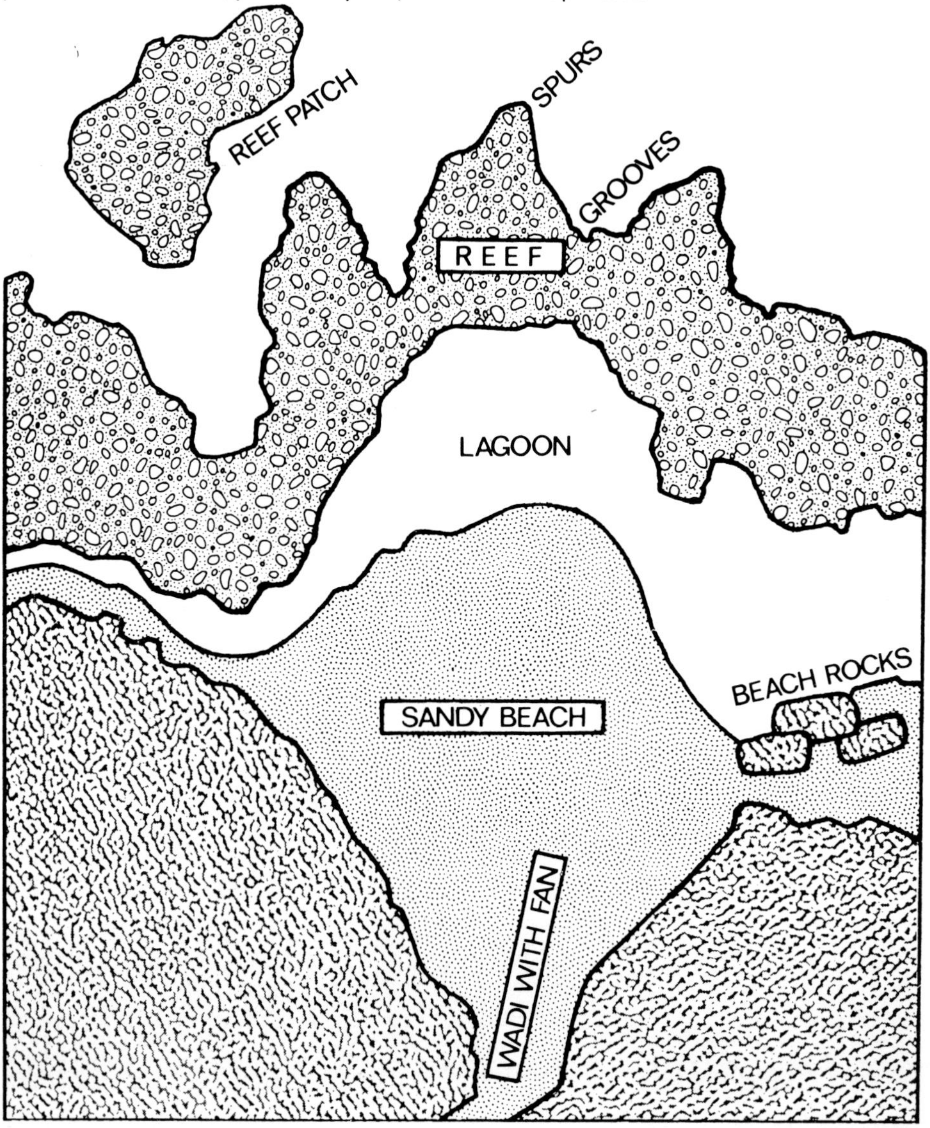

Beach Rock: built from a geological debris carried from the mainland to the shore or from coral debris and other organic material: held together in a conglomerate by carbonation.

Lagoon: a shallow water zone between the shore and reef table, generally with sandy bottom supporting grasses, sea weed and small clumps of coral.

Reef Table: a flat table in shallow water and, therefore, influenced by tide and wave action. (Reef tables may create difficulties for divers when seeking open water, particularly when the table is very wide and shallow.)

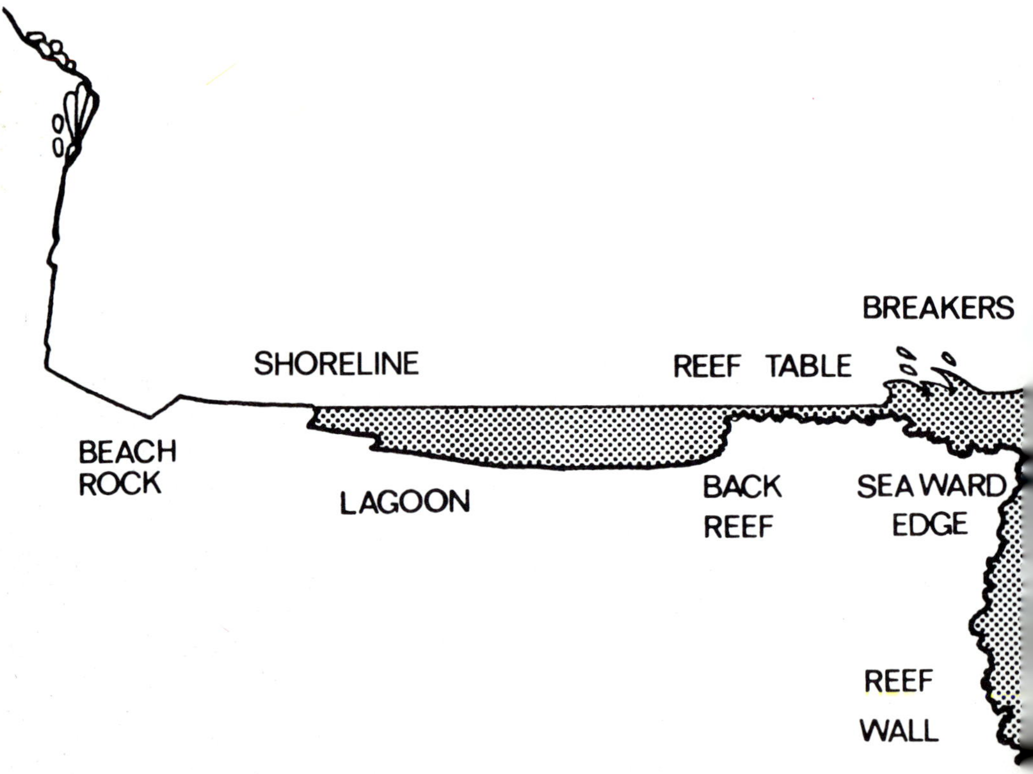

Seaward Edge: where the coral descends from the table vertically or in steps – this is the richest section of the reef ecology, particularly where there are steps. Coral dwellers and open water species meet and mingle at the seaward edge and the diver finds rugged terrain with crevices, caves and grottoes providing the most rewarding diving locations.

Reef Wall: the open sea wall descending more rapidly, often vertically, from the seaward edge with, of course, a gradual thinning out of flora and fauna at greater depths.

Sand Slope: ranging from horizontal to vertical bottom depending upon the location, supporting grasses, sea weed and coral clumps.

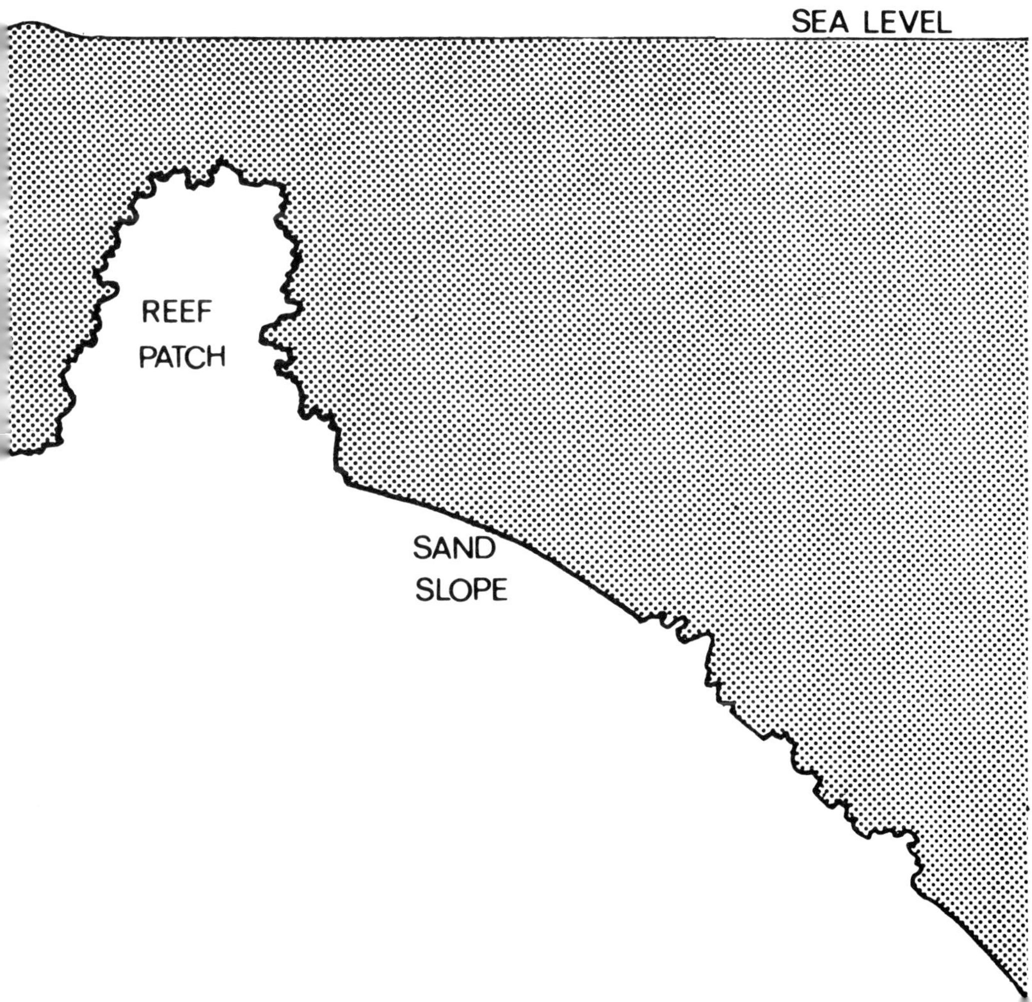

The Beduin

More than 10,000 Beduin inhabit Sinai with about ten tribes divided into two major groups.

The Muzeini, known as the largest and most powerful, is a tribe of more than two-thousand. They reached Sinai from Saudia Arabia about 400 years ago. However, the most ancient Beduin tribe in the peninsula is the Jebalya, having arrived in the 6th century. They have a fascinating history. In 532 Justinian brought pagan worshippers from the Black Sea area, in what is Rumania today, to guard and serve the monks at the Monastery of Santa Katerina. This foundation of the Jebalya tribe converted gradually to Christianity and were followers of that faith until the end of the Byzantine Period. Following the Moslem conquests of the 7th century and their total isolation, they became Moslems. Numbering more than 1,100 today, they are the best educated Beduin in Sinai and most adult males know how to read and write.

Beduin society is patriarchal and they consider themselves subject only to the law of the tribe. The highest political and social authority, the tribe, is called "Kabila" in Arabic while each successive generation is classified in the social and lineal hierarchy as a separate unit. The lowest social unit is, of course, the family. The ruler of the tribe, the "Sheikh", was in the past traditionally chosen by inherited blood line but today power and inner intrigue determines this leadership.

The unique and isolated way-of-life of the Beduin has created an equally unique and special tradition. To them if you are not a Beduin, even though a local resident, you are a "stranger". To receive fairness and honor from them demands the same from you *and this is the key to your contacts with them.*

Please take note that burial monuments of the Sheikhs, surrounded by guest huts known as "makad" in Arabic, are holy places so respect them as such. You may also find Beduin caches in desert trees where they keep their possessions, placing them there and not returning for long periods of time. **Therefore, remember, everything you may discover in the desert has, in the Beduin's eyes, both ownership and honor: a deserted hut, a wandering camel, old rags and clothes, a jerrycan, etc. Do not occupy, touch or take.**

DIVING IN SINAI

Sinai is a diver's wonderland — but, like Alice, you need the right key to get in! The following summarizes procedures for individuals wishing to enter Sinai. (All information courtesy of Neot Hakikar Safari Ltd. Tel: (059) 71329, 76908. Prices quoted are those in effect at the time of publication and are subject to change).

USING PUBLIC TRANSPORT

Take bus number 15 to Taba from the Central Bus Station or from the offices of Neot Hakikar in Eilat. Once at Taba, go to the border checkpoint where your passport will be stamped. Then you will be provided with transport to the Egyptian border. Egyptian buses leave Taba for Nuweiba, Dahab, Sharm El Sheikh and Santa Katerina twice daily at 10:00 and 14:00.

BY PRIVATE CAR

You may enter Sinai in a private car if it is registered in your name. If the vehicle is registered in someone else's name, or if it is a hired vehicle, you need either proof of ownership in the first instance, or, in the second case, power of attorney stating explicitly that permission has been granted to take the vehicle over the border to Egypt. Commercial vehicles, diesel and four wheel drive vehicles are not permitted, nor are jeeps. You will have to present a translation of your driver's licence — translations are available from MEMSI.

After stamping your passport at the Taba customs checkpoint, proceed to the Egyptian side. Here you will fill out an entry form. Then pass through customs and pay $6 Egyptian port tax before crossing the border. In addition, you will have to pay $28 per vehicle for customs, new plates and insurance. This insurance covers the driver of the vehicle only, in the event that he or she injures a local citizen. It does not cover vehicle damage or theft. Passengers of private vehicles are also subject to all the requirements listed below.

DOCUMENTATION NEEDED AND PROCEDURES

Every tourist wishing to enter Sinai is required to have a passport valid for at least six months. On the Israeli side you pay port tax of 13 NIS, fill out an exit form and have your passport stamped. Any photographic or diving equipment must be declared at customs.

Israelis please note that you need an army release form for visiting the Sinai. If you hold two passports, you need to carry your Israeli passport with you.

Foreign passport holders must present the form filled out on arrival in Israel. Note that if any of your children appear in your passport, you will not be allowed to cross the border without that child!

On the Egyptian side, you need to declare any photographic or diving equipment and to pay $6 port tax to the Egyptians when proceeding through customs. SPEAR GUNS ARE NOT ALLOWED THROUGH CUSTOMS.

The visa you will receive at the border is for 7 days (6 nights) ONLY. If you return later than the date allowed, you will have to pay a fine of $35, and you will experience difficulties should you attempt to visit the Sinai on subsequent occasions!

If you wish to visit the Sinai for a period longer than 7 days, you will need an Egyptian visa. When passing through the Taba checkpoint, state that you are carrying an Egyptian visa, as you require a different stamp from the one granted visitors up to 7 days. In addition, your passport must be stamped within 7 days of your being in the Sinai at the Egyptian police. If you fail to have your passport stamped, you will have to pay a fine of $35 when leaving!

All visitors must declare the amount of money they are bringing into Egypt at customs, and must receive an appropriate declaration form.

DIVING EQUIPMENT

It is possible to hire equipment and to obtain refills and diving-related services at Dahab and at Sharm El Sheikh. It is advisable, though, to bring your equipment with you from Israel and to use local facilities for refills etc. Remember, no spear guns!

That concludes your Red Sea red tape — enjoy your trip!

THE DIVING SITES

TO BEGIN

The following locations were chosen to give you the widest possible spectrum of diving experiences in the Gulf. This selection gives dive plans varying in their challenge to enthusiasts: a specific locale on the reef; areas for extended exploration; marinescapes in shallow or deep water, or both; with or without a boat (the majority are easily accessible with a standard passenger vehicle); a few require extra stamina and experience. For the convenience of friends and family on the trip who are not divers, sites also providing a rich experience with just mask, fins and snorkel are marked with an asterisk.

DIVING AREA

Eilat

1. North Beach Wreck
2. Japanese Gardens & Moses Rock
3. The Caves*
4. Taba*
5. Coral Island*
6. Sun Pool*
7. Marsa el-Muqabila
8. Ras Burka

Dahab

9. Southern Oasis
10. The Canyon
11. Nakab Shaheen
12. The Lighthouse*

Nabek

13. Nahalat el-Tel*
14. The Maria Schröder
15. Shora el-Manqata

Ras Muhammed

16. The Quay
17. Shark Reef (boat)
18. Shark Observatory

Key to Symbols

1. Entry

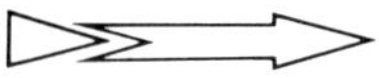

2. Snorkeling

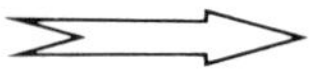

3. Dive

4. Ascend

5. Underwater route

6. Breakers

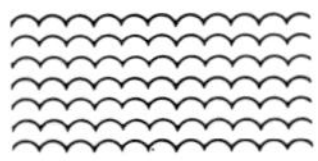

7. Shallows — no passage by snorkeling

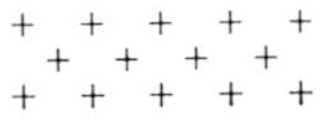

8. Photographic site and direction of view

9. Depth in meters

35

10. Indicating North

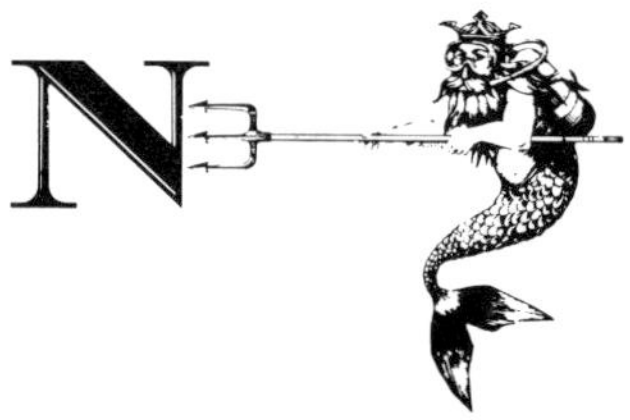

11. Good for exploration

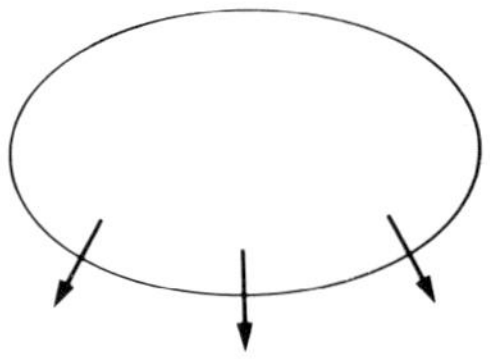

12. Land Approach

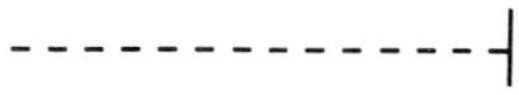

GULF OF EILAT 1:250,000

EL KARNUS
EL HIBEK
GULF OF EILAT
RAS ABU GALUM
WADI DAHAB
DAHAB
DI-ZAHAV
11
10
12
9
82
80
78
77
76

DAHAB
12
DI-ZAHAV
9
760
SHARIRA PASS
750
WADI KABILA
740
GULF OF EILAT
SHORA
15
EL-MANQATA
14
PALM TREE JUNCTION
(REF: 09447336)
WADI KID
730
13
EL ARKANA
NABEK
720
HEY DAROMA
(WRECK)
STRAITS OF TIRAN
JACKSON REEF
GORDON REEF
TIRAN ISLAND
RAS NASRANI
710

KEY

- BORDER
- RAILROAD
- OIL PIPELINE
- CONTOUR IN METERS
- ALTITUDE IN METERS
- FIRST CLASS ROAD
- SECOND CLASS ROAD
- GOOD UNPAVED ROAD
- UNPAVED ROAD
- DESERT TRACK
- RIVER
- WADI
- WATER CHANNEL
- CLIFFS
- VERTICAL SLOPE
- TOWN
- VILLAGE
- PLACE NAME OR BUILDING
- MOSQUE OR SHEIKH BURIAL
- CHURCH OR MONASTERY
- TEL (MOUND)
- CASTLE
- MINE
- LIGHTHOUSE
- AIRPORT
- SPRING, WELL OR WATERHOLE
- MUD
- SUBJECT TO FLOODING
- SALT FLAT
- SAND

HOW TO READ THE DIVE

Route No. 101 — look for the route number in the list of sites to find the general diving area.

Ref: 12345678 — these numbers give the coordinates to find the exact location on your regional Israel map.

11°22′33″E 44°55′66″N — the exact latitude and longtitude for the site on your international charts.

Departure: Excitement City — the most convenient starting point(s) for driving to the dive and the total distance to the site.

Road Condition & Route: South by air — the direction, surface road condition(s) and, rarely necessary, type of vehicle required.

The Map
This map is a section of the Israel regional map for southern Sinai in this book and provides you with local roads and tracks, distances, topography, coastline, habitations, etc. at the diving site.

The text here will give you careful directions and information concerning the location and how to find the best dive there. Special notes may advise or caution, guaranteeing a more comfortable, safer, or easier dive. Whenever necessary, depending upon the site, this section will provide all the more detailed instruction, both terrestrial and marine, to ensure that you find what you are looking for.

Schematic Drawing of the Site
This general cross-cut illustration of the reef area is not a map but an overall impression of the marine topography you will encounter at the site, helping you plan your dives there.

The Photographs
You will find photographs here of terrestrial and marine landmarks either aiding in recognition of the way to the site or pointing out a particular marine locale good for pictures.

EILAT

Eilat is unique among Israel's cities and is one of the most unusual urban centers in the world. Located at the tip of the Gulf of Eilat, the city stands on the Great Continental Rift that divides Africa and Asia, and is a crossroads to Israel, Jordan, Egypt and Saudia Arabia. Although a settlement existed here in biblical times, modern Eilat was founded in the second half of this century by an assortment of characters out of a Wild West scenario — dreamy-eyed idealists, adventurers, rousters and job- seekers — willing to bear the 40°C (104°F) temperatures, to live in tents and shacks, to ration their water and to depend on a fragile, haphazard air service for their link with those "up north". The diverse origins of these pioneers — hailing from London, Los Angeles, Paris, Tangiers, Baghdad, Bombay and all points in between — are matched only by the natural diversities of the city's surroundings. Eilat is a harmonious conjunction of tropical sea, rugged barren mountains and desert valleys, perfectly balanced so that none of these elements is overpowering.

Although Eilat retains its colorful cosmopolitanism, today its character is sophisticated rather than spartan. Its 24 000 residents live in modern, airconditioned apartments and are employed in enterprises as varied as tourism, mining, jewelry, ceramics, fishing and shipping. No longer an isolated pioneer town, Eilat is about four hours by road — or fifty minutes by air — from Tel Aviv and Jerusalem. The terminal at the international airport bang in the middle of town, between the shopping centers on the one hand and the luxury beach-hotels on the other, is a modern airconditioned version of the legendary stagecoach station — filled with a curious mixture of tourists, mothers and babies, construction workers, soldiers, loafers, businessmen, chess players and tourist guides. And, of course, the usual divers, loaded with equipment, arriving from Zurich or Goteborg or London or Chicago or Tel Aviv or....

Eilat's development over the last few years has been stupendous, with new luxury hotels and attractive shopping malls springing up like so many glistening glass corals. In the wake of the Israel- Egypt Peace Treaty and the return of the Sinai to Egypt, Eilat is without doubt the major tourist mecca of the region. Its facilities include helpful tourist bureaux, restaurants catering for all tastes from fast-foods to cordon bleu cuisine, shopping and banking, a police station, a hospital and of course vibrant entertainment with bars, nightclubs, cafes and discos galore.

Accommodation ranges from youth hostels, holiday villages and campsites to fine five star hotels. The North Beach of Eilat is a self-contained resort area consisting of the world renowned King Solomon's Palace Hotel, with its elegant French Brasserie restaurant, English-style Yacht Pub and new Sheba Disco. Nearby, you will find the Lagoona Hotel, a luxury, four-star hotel, and the Sport Hotel — aptly named as it caters for every sport imaginable. The King's Wharf Shopping Center was recently opened on the lagoon in front of the Lagoona and King Solomon's Palace hotels. It features restaurants, cafes, a pub, a new disco, the head office of the Red Sea Sports Club, a boutique, photo shop, jewelry shop, and the newly opened Paris-style department store — Le Drugstore — where you can purchase everything from shoelaces to diamonds.

Clearly, your non-diving travel companions need not be bored for even the fraction of a second! Should the delights of shopping and waterside cafes pall, there is always the option of the Country Club which offers the entire spectrum of major sports facilities, two jaccuzis and a sauna. Alternatively, tour agencies with the finest equipment and professional guides can take the adventurous into the sea, desert or mountains for half a day or a month if so desired! Car rental firms provide standard passenger cars, minibuses, jeeps or command cars for desert safaris. And while you are admiring the intricate treasures of the spectacular coral gardens, your beloved can admire the delicate oriental filigree, lapis lazuli, turquoise, pearl and Eilat stone creations of Malkit — specialist Eilat jewellers.

Eilat's ever-growing tourist trade received added impetus in 1985 when the city was designated a free-trading zone. Widespread trade and tax concessions have come into effect in the Zone which includes Eilat, Kibbutz Eilot and Taba Beach. The prices of commodities and services are effectively reduced by 15% — which means you get that much more for your money! Visitors entering and leaving Eilat are reminded that the same laws apply to the Free Trading Zone for Customs and Duty Purposes as apply to international travel to and from Israel.

Eilat's special attraction is, undoubtedly, the sea. The prevailing northerlies funneled to Eilat from the great Rift's Arava Valley create a remarkable phenomenon: a tropical sea in the midst of an arid desert climate. Your dive planning for the Eilat area will be trouble-free as everything a diver needs is freely available. Its results are certain to be most rewarding. One point is important to stress. Diving south along the Gulf is no more expensive than taking a jaunt to the Caribbean or Central America. Although transport to Israel is more expensive, these costs are balanced out by the relatively inexpensive costs of accommodation and diving facilities. European divers need no persuading about Eilat's advantages — and arrive here in great numbers every year.

Eilat's sunshine, blue water and clear skies ensure your diving enjoyment — but don't forget to drink plenty of soft, liquid refreshment to avoid dehydration!

DISTANCES

Coral Beach - Marsa El-Muqabila 26KM. (16 MI).
Marsa El-Muqabila - Ras Burka 24KM. (15 MI).
Ras Burka - Nuweiba 20KM. (12.4 MI).

NORTH BEACH

★★★★ SHULAMIT GARDENS HOTEL
Airport
★★★★ GALEI EILAT HOTEL
KING
★★ BEL HOTEL
★★★★ CAESAR
★★★★ MORIAH EILAT HOTEL
★★★★ NEPTUNE HOTEL
Marina

★★★ AMERICANA HOTEL
★★★ MOON VALLEY HOTEL
KINGS WHARF SHOPPING CENTER
★★★★ KING SOLOMON'S PALACE HOTEL
ON'S RED SEA
MARINA
★★★★ LAGOONA HOTEL
★★★★ QUEEN OF SHEBA HOTEL
ST. TROPEZ HOTEL
★★★ SPORT HOTEL
Jordanian Border
RED SEA SPORTS CLUB

U GO!

EUROCARD
MasterCard
MC

CORAL BEACH

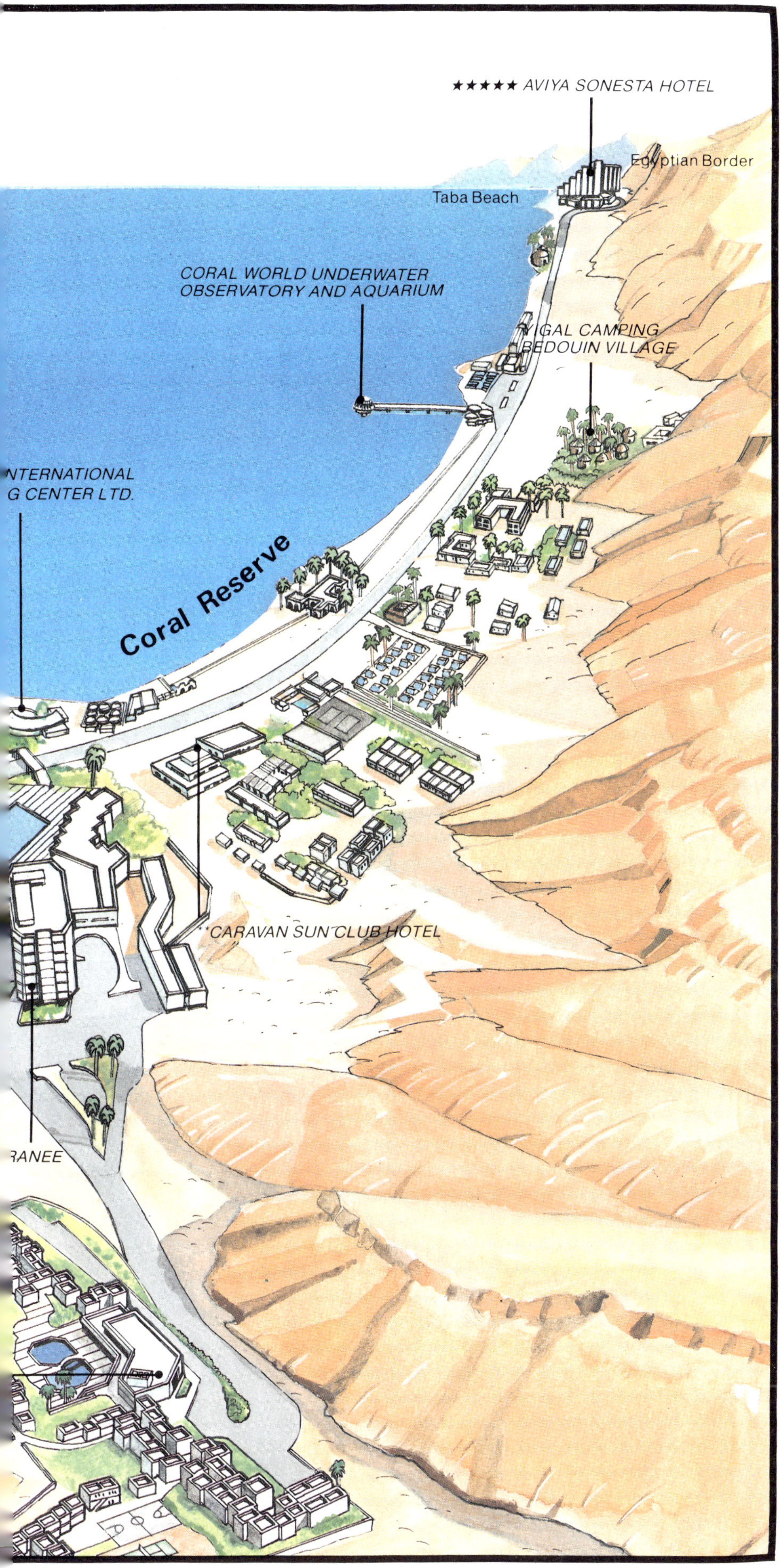
★★★★★ AVIYA SONESTA HOTEL
Egyptian Border
Taba Beach
CORAL WORLD UNDERWATER
OBSERVATORY AND AQUARIUM
YIGAL CAMPING
BEDOUIN VILLAGE
NTERNATIONAL
G CENTER LTD.
Coral Reserve
**CARAVAN SUN CLUB HOTEL
RANEE

NORTH BEACH WRECK

Route No.1
Ref: 14528845
34°57′10″E 29°32′30″N
Departure & Route: Located directly at the southern exit from Eilat.

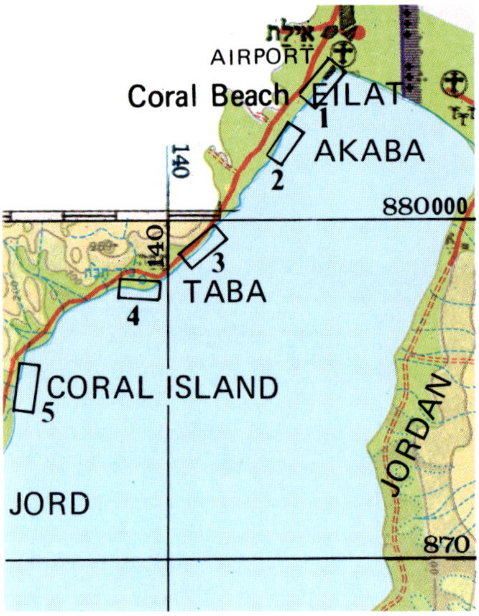

This is a well-known diving site — the only one actually situated in the city itself. It was one of the standard attractions in the early days of diving in Eilat.

Both the name and the past of the wreck situated here are unknown, and to tell the truth, not much is left of it. But this is an easy dive, and very conveniently located. It is easy to identify, about 100m. after the junction at the southern exit from Eilat. Enter the water using the concrete slope next to the palm tree (B). It is important to descend left of the line of buoys, and to proceed in a straight line towards the silo across the bay.

Fragments of the wreck (A) rest on the flat, sandy ocean bottom at a depth of 20m., and at a distance of about 50m. from the beach. Large bush-like white corals (Acroporal) interspersed with soft corals are to be found in the area. Watch out for windsurfers!

A

B

EILAT AIRPORT
N
TO CORAL BEACH
B
A
6
10
20
20

EILAT AIRPORT
TO CORAL BEACH
6
10
20
20

THE ENDLESS SEATIME

THE CAVES

Route No. 3*
Ref: 14138791
34°54′40′′E 29°29′30′′N
Departure: From Aquasport, 2km. south on the road to Taba.

A

B

This site is located right next to the road between the university and Taba. Because of its proximity to the road, access is very easy.

Drive towards Taba until the little lighthouse on the hill to the right of the road (some people call this site "The Lighthouse"). Enter the sea south of the rocks which are clearly seen on the beachfront (B).

The dive takes you to a reef, surrounded by a sandy ocean floor. The shallow water makes easy access to the many cracks and caves which fissure the rock (A).

The Caves are recommended for beginners in underwater photography and are a good place to practise your techniques. The cave-dwelling Rased Fish is a characteristic resident of this location (see Fish Index).

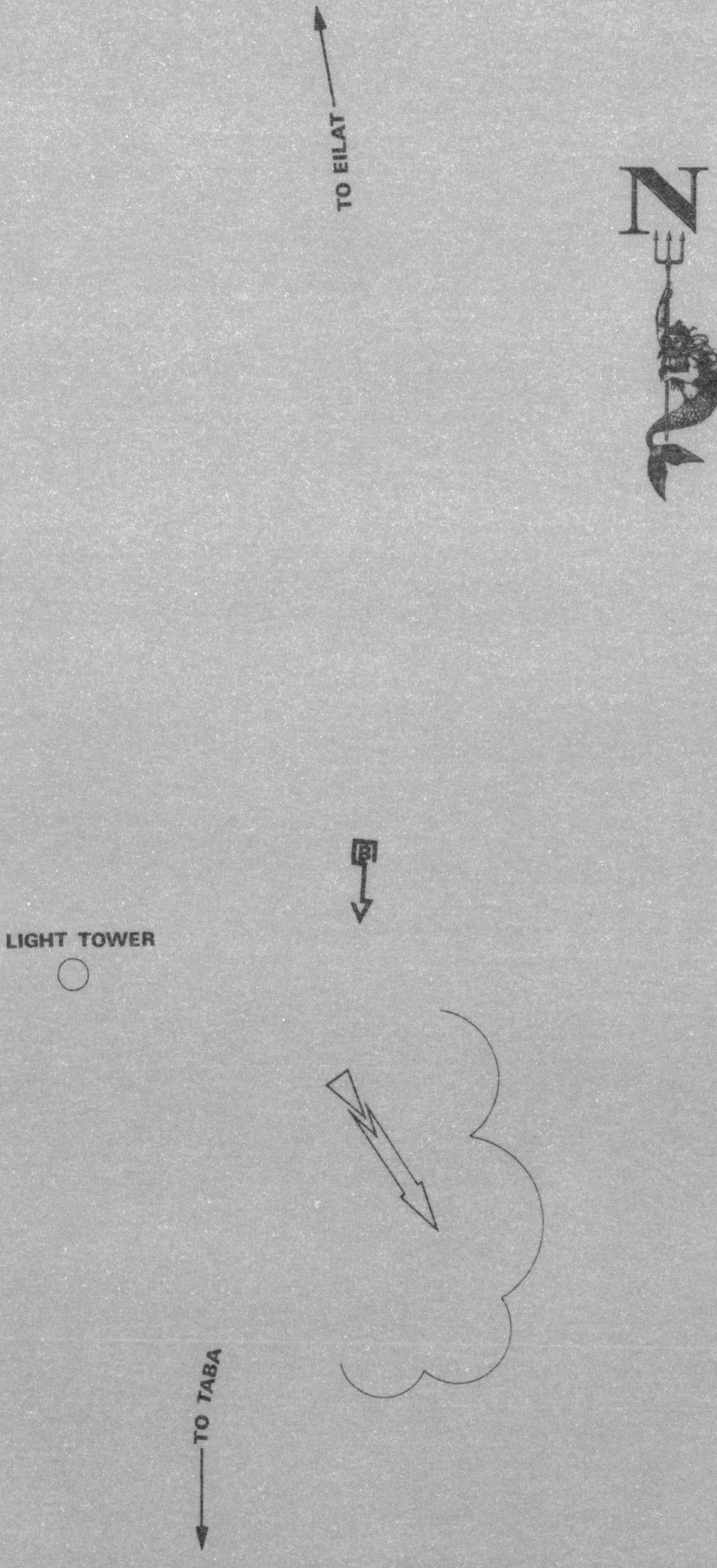

TO EILAT
N
LIGHT TOWER
B
TO TABA

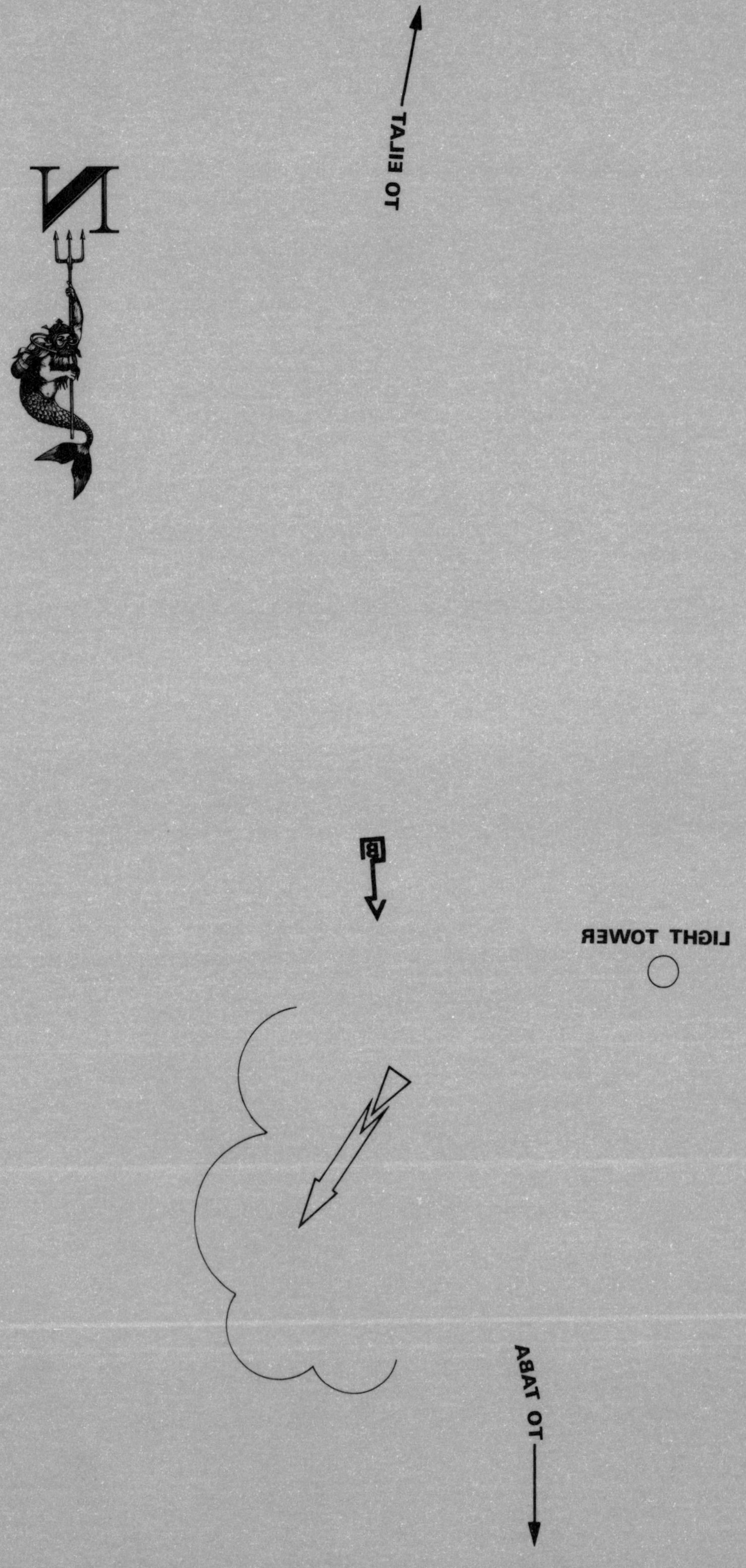

TO EILAT
N
B
LIGHT TOWER
TO TABA

JAPANESE GARDENS

Route No. 2*

Ref: 14328820
34°56′30″E 29°31′00″N
Departure & Route: Directly in front of Aqua Sport Diving Centre – two minutes on foot.

This is the most familiar and well known site in the Eilat area. Most divers arriving at the Gulf for the first time start their exploration of the area here. The Japanese Gardens, a nature reserve, begins near the diving center and extends south to the marine tower observatory (one of four in the world). Moses Rock rests a short distance off the reef table from the gardens and, therefore, it is more convenient planning two approaches at this location, starting with the rock.

Moses Rock

Enter the sea in front of the diving center and dive due east. By finning quietly and gently to a point about 30 m. (100 ft.) from the shore you will discover a Garden Eel community (see FISH INDEX), just at the beginning of a steep sandy slope in 4 m. (13.2 ft.) depth. Turn due south and fin along the slope at exactly 6 m. (20 ft.) depth to arrive at Moses Rock in 15–20 minutes. The rock is submerged from near sea-level to sandy bottom at 6–8 m. (20–26 ft.) and a regular habitat for a wide variety of fish totally unafraid of divers. They will immediately surround you, waiting to be fed (take along a bit of bread). For a return, dive due west from the rock to the reef table and then fin north along the coral back to the diving center.

If you prefer snorkeling directly to Moses Rock from the diving center, take a compass reading of 170° and you will arrive at the site with about 15 minutes of average finning.

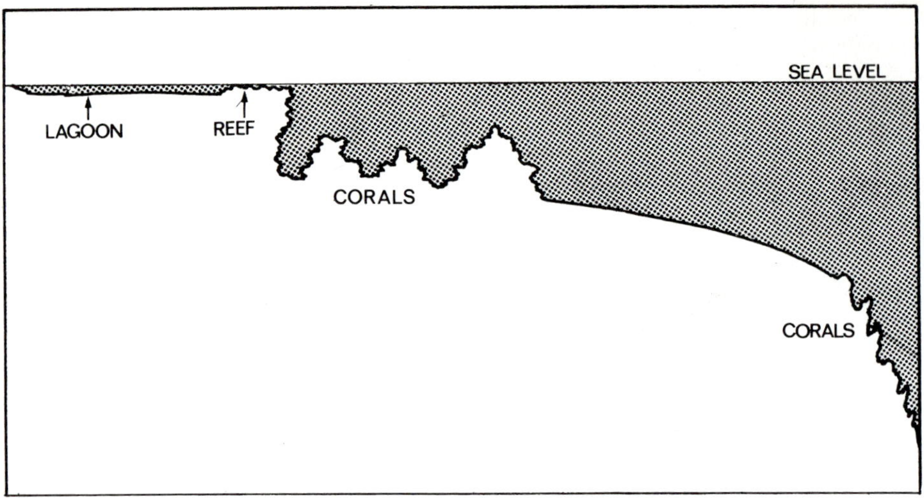

Japanese Gardens

Looking at the schematic drawing of the coral system at this site you will recognize a formation of coral knolls resting on sandy slope: ranging from about 4 m. (13.2 ft.) depth next to the reef table to 15–45 m. (50–150 ft.) depth about 50–70 m. (165–231 ft.) east of the reef. You have two options for a good dive plan: 1) explore the area of the reef, or 2) plan a deep dive.

Your first option is to explore the gardens along the seaward edge of the table as a separate dive. The second possibility is to continue down the sandy slope to the deeper gardens and then decompress next to the reef at the end of your dive.

Special Note: Although relatively narrow the table is difficult to cross so study your aerial photograph and choose the most convenient entry for your particular plan.

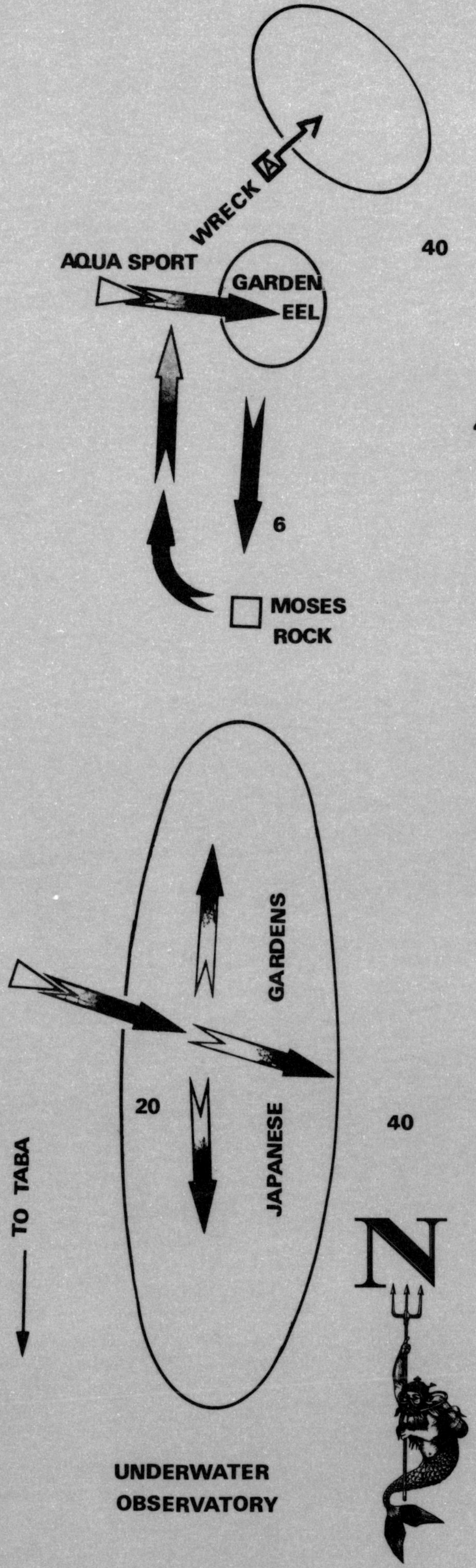
WRECK
AQUA SPORT
GARDEN
EEL
40
40
6
MOSES
ROCK
GARDENS
JAPANESE
20
40
TO TABA
N
UNDERWATER
OBSERVATORY

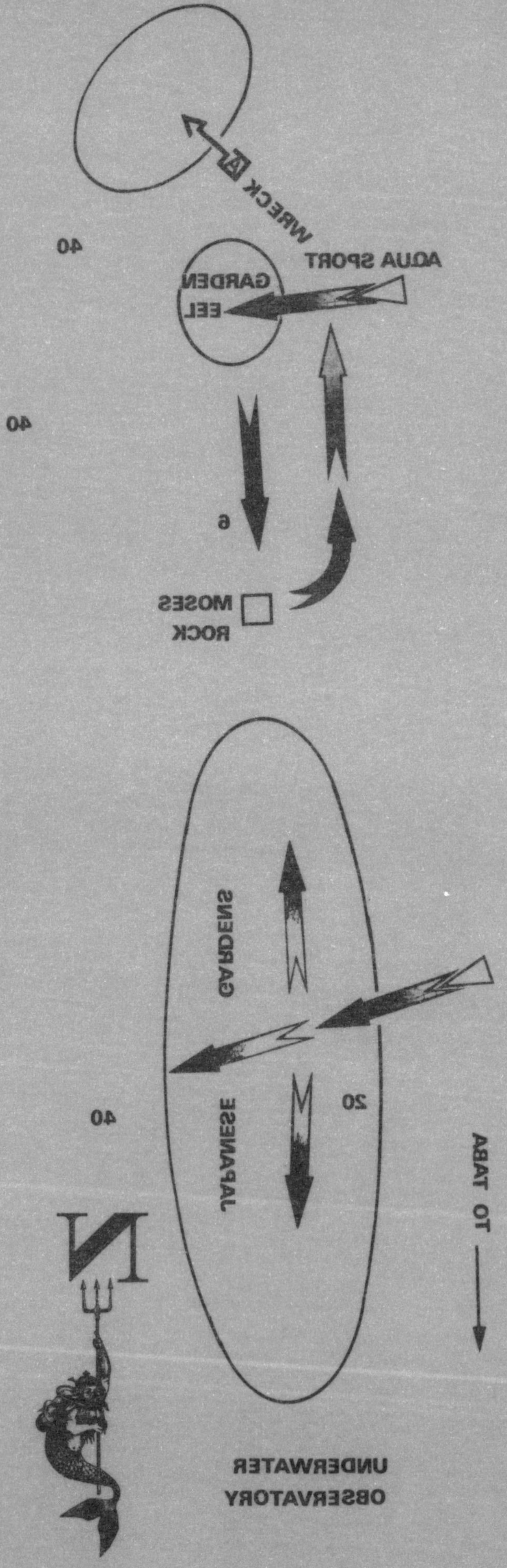
WRECK
AQUA SPORT
GARDEN
EEL
40
40
6
MOSES
ROCK
JAPANESE
GARDENS
20
40
TO TABA
UNDERWATER
OBSERVATORY
N

TABA

Route No. 4*
Ref: 13988780
34°53′30″E 29°29′36″N
Departure: **Coral Beach** – 3.6 km. (2.3 mi.)
Road Condition & Route: South on the road to Ophira with good asphalt followed by 300 m. (1,000 ft.) of unpaved road.

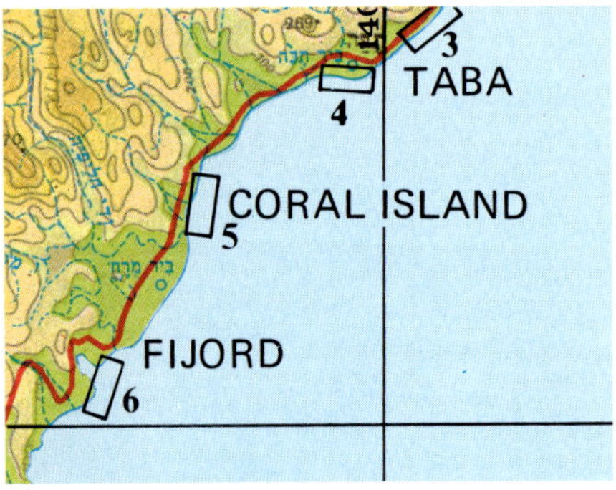

The northern edge of Taba Bay is marked by a prominent solitary hill. Driving south from **Coral Beach** watch carefully for the stone marking kilometer 181. Turn left off the main highway at this marker and continue on the beach road to Rafi Nelson's Village nestling directly behind that hill on the sea shore (A). Park your vehicle at his gate and walk or snorkel about 80 m. (264 ft.) southwest along the shore of the bay until you see an underwater rift near a few reef patches. The first break between these patches leads to a reef 40 m. (132 ft.) below (B). Dive along the north side of the patches to find the break leading down to the rift. The south side of the rift itself is sandy slope, often with sting rays, so dive parallel to and a bit south of the patches down to the reef.

There is food, drink, music and swimming at the Village during the day.

A

B

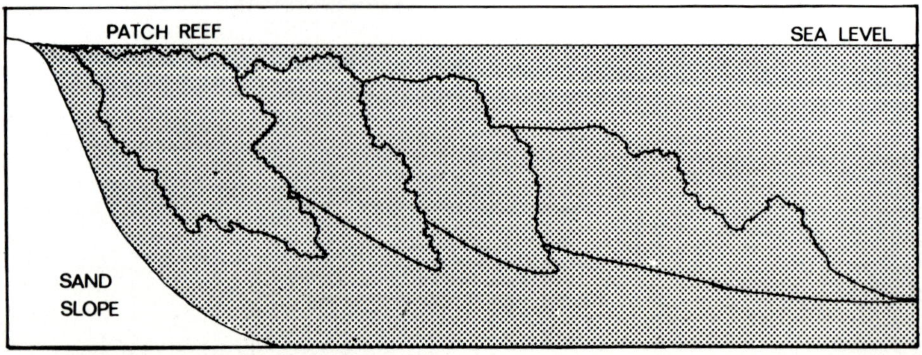

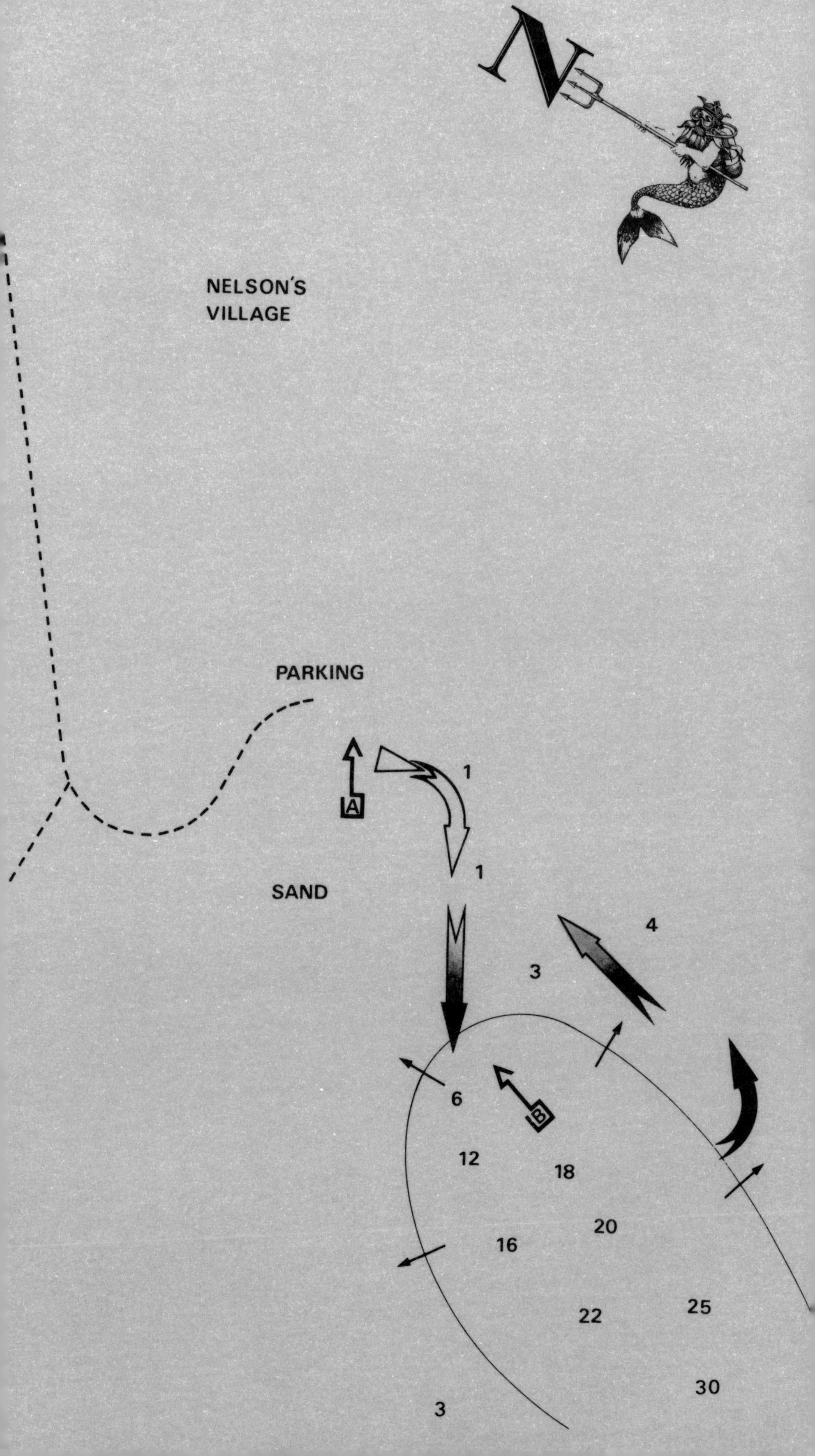
N
NELSON'S VILLAGE
PARKING
A
1
1
SAND
4
3
6
B
12
18
20
16
22
25
30
3

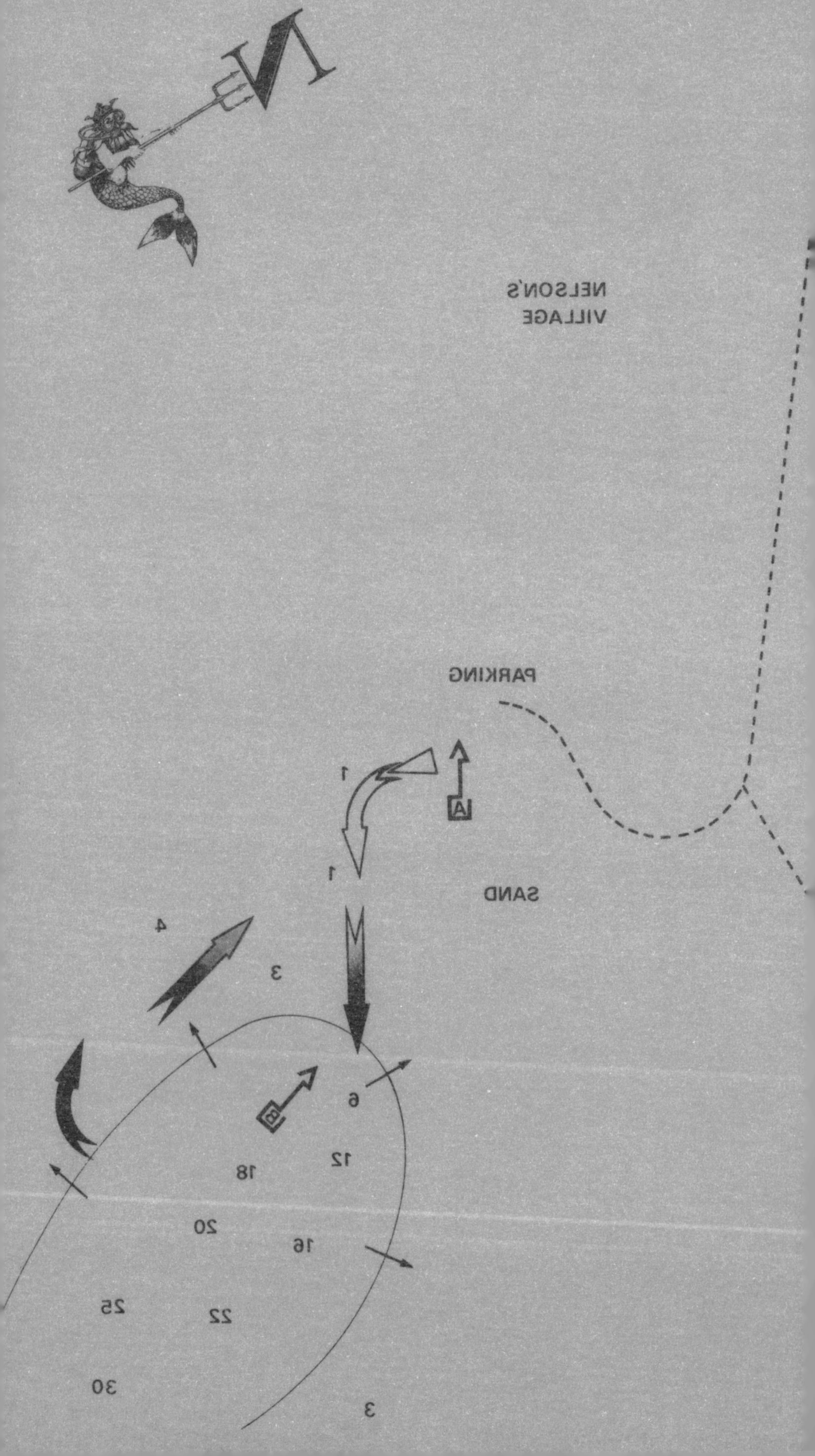

N
NELSON'S
VILLAGE
PARKING
A
1
1
SAND
4
3
B
6
12
18
20
16
25
22
30
3

CORAL ISLAND

Route No. 5 *

Ref: 13628748
34°51′40″E 20°27′30″N
Departure: **Coral Beach** 17 kms. (10.5 mi.)
Road Conditions & Route: South on road to Sharm el Sheikh. Good asphalt.

A shallow-water reef, which runs parallel to the Sinai shore at a distance of 10 meters. The distance to Coral Island, across the channel from the closest point, is 220 m. (726 ft.). The island itself is 350 m. (1,155 ft.) long and 150 m. wide. You will find an impressive Crusader fortress on the island, built approx. 1115 A.D. Note the ceilings, reinforced with palm logs, the huge fresh-water reservoirs, (no water supply on the island), the Slit-windows for defence, and the bases of sunken columns in the salt-water pond. The site was inhabited in the Byzantine, Crusader and Muslem periods. There is evidence of Bronze Age culture. You will find soft drinks and public facilities at the beach "Kiosk" during the tourist season.

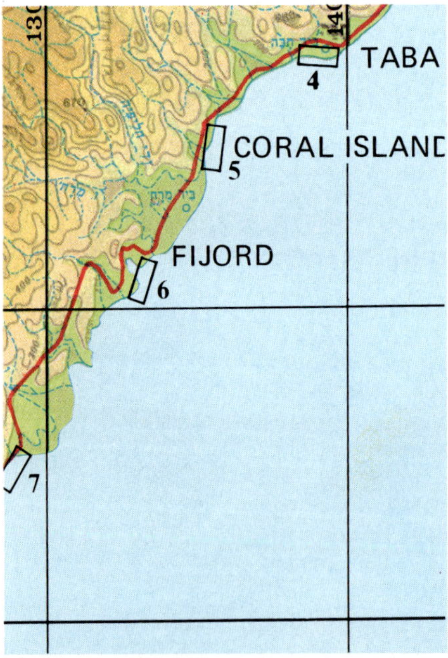

Dive plan: You can cross the reef, but preferably you should enter the channel through the break in the lagoon directly under the quay.

Snorkel across to the southern half of the island, 270 m. (890 ft.) from where you are standing, utilizing the gentle southerly current. (If you prefer to dive across and explore the floor, your depths will range from 10 to 17 m.). When you reach the island, dive in a south-easterly direction around the reef surrounding it, until you reach the island landing stage. From there you can return to your starting point. Decompressing at 3 m. (10 ft.) circling the island itself and returning to the quay takes about 75 minutes of uninterrupted average finning.

A boat service from the shore to the island is generally available. This naturally gives you more time to explore the reef, and conserves energy for exploration.

A →

B →

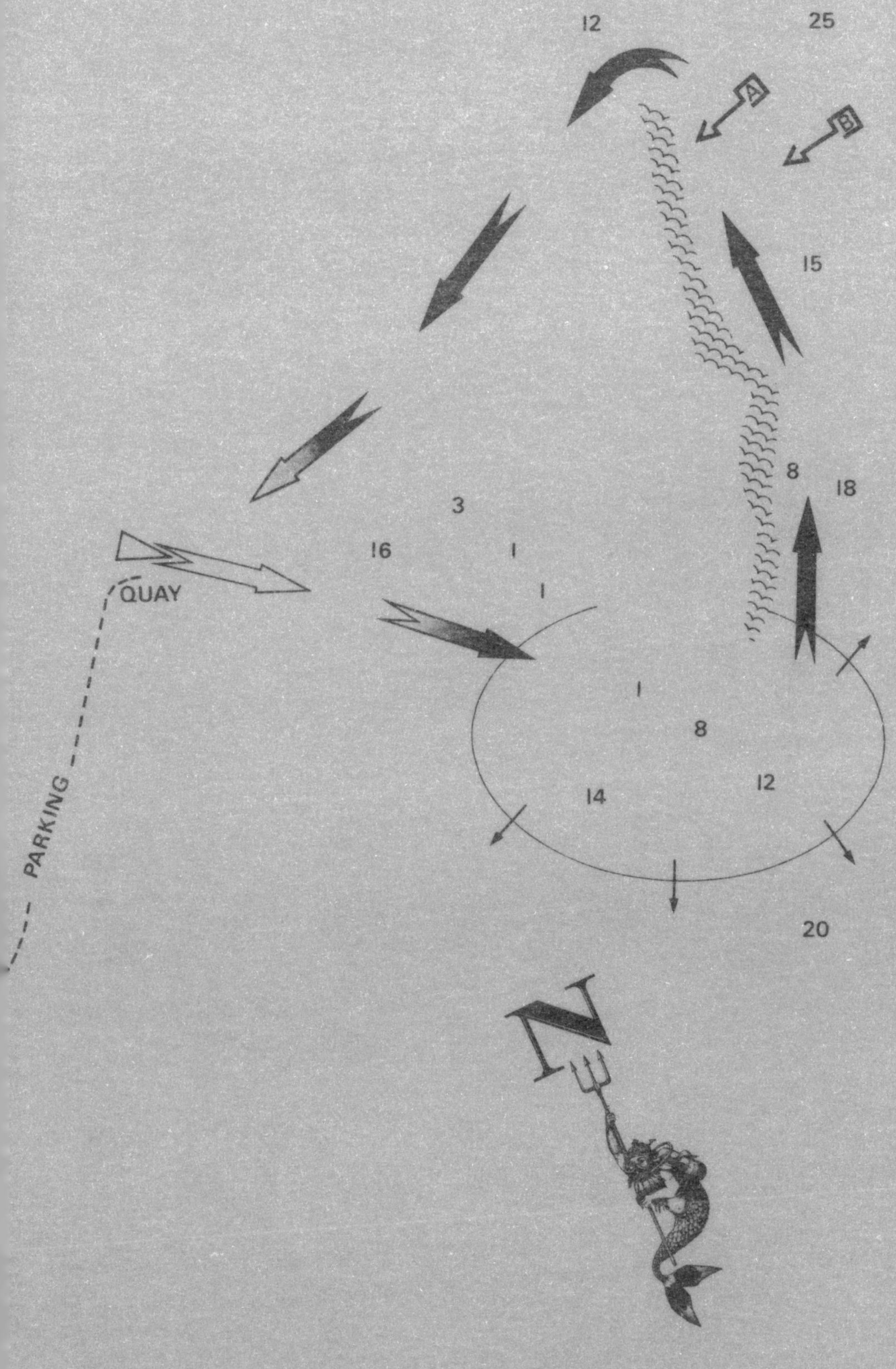
12
25
A
B
15
8
18
3
16
1
1
QUAY
1
8
12
14
PARKING
20
N

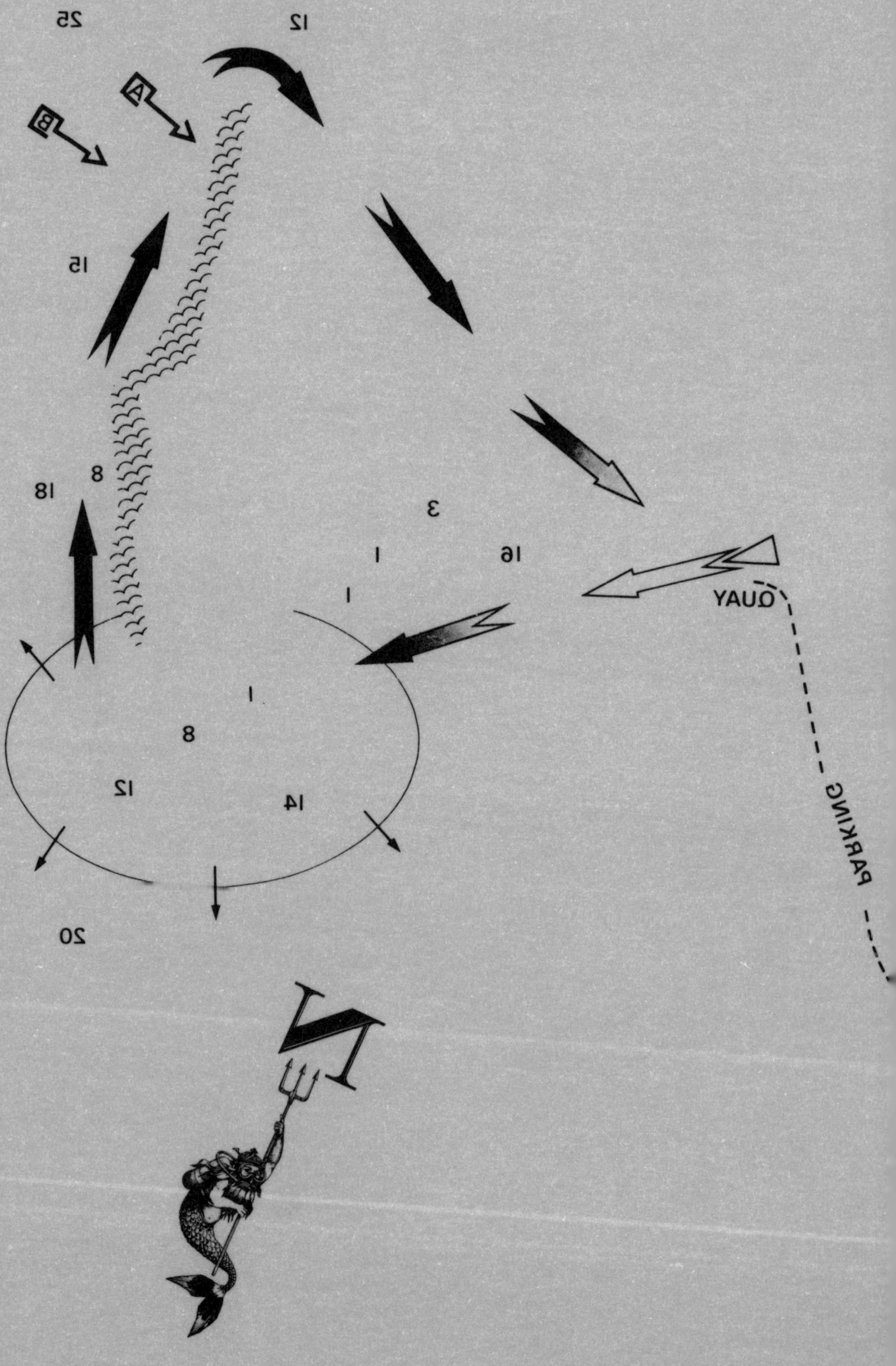
QUAY
PARKING
12
25
A
B
15
8
18
3
16
1
1
1
8
12
14
20
N

SUN POOL

Route No. 6*
Ref: 13308704
34°49'30"E 29°25'30"N
Departure: **Coral Beach** – 17.7 km. (12 mi.)
Road Condition & Route: South on the road to Ophira with good asphalt followed by 700 m. (2,310 ft.) of unpaved road.

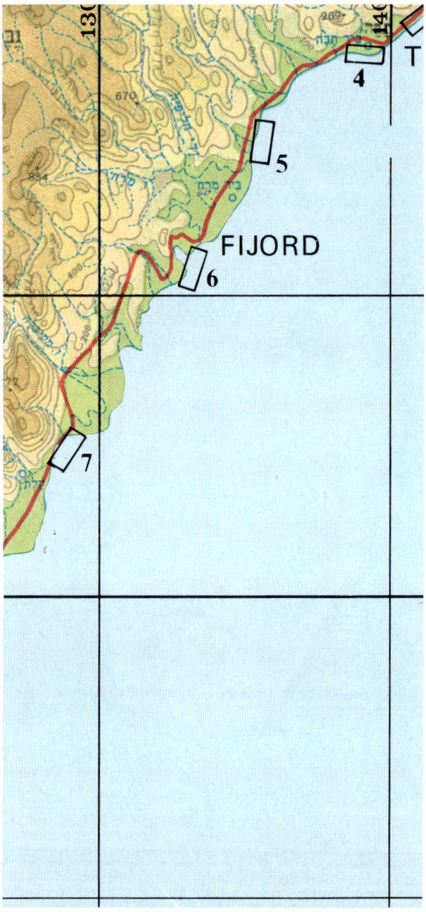

Turn left off the main highway after passing the Fijord. (Not the road down to the Fijord.) The road circles back around a hill till it reaches the seashore and is heading north in the direction of the Fijord entrance. Continue on this unpaved road until you are stopped by huge boulders blocking the way. Begin your dive at this point and fin along the seaward wall of the reef north as it parallels the shore to the mouth of the Fijord. At the point of your entry the reef reaches 4 m. (13.2 ft.) depth and continuing north it bottoms at 12 m. (40 ft.) until it terminates at the mouth of the Fijord. Explore the area of the mouth and you will discover several reefs. You can shorten your dive and save air by walking to the Fijord entrance but it is rough going along rocky shore.

Don't forget to take a stroll beyond the boulders to the Sun Pool, an interesting geological phenomenon. To preserve its natural beauty swimming is not permitted there.

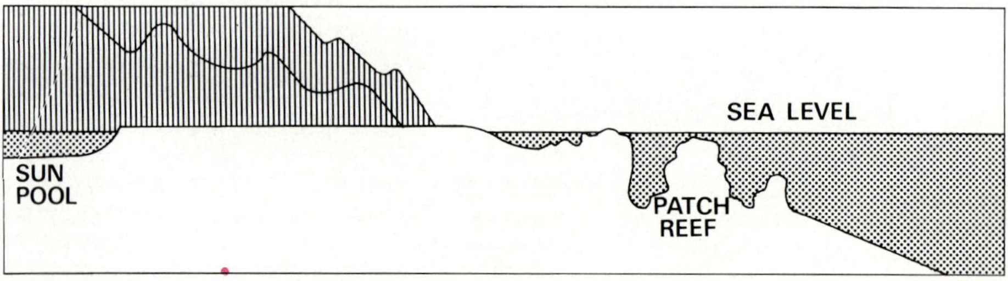

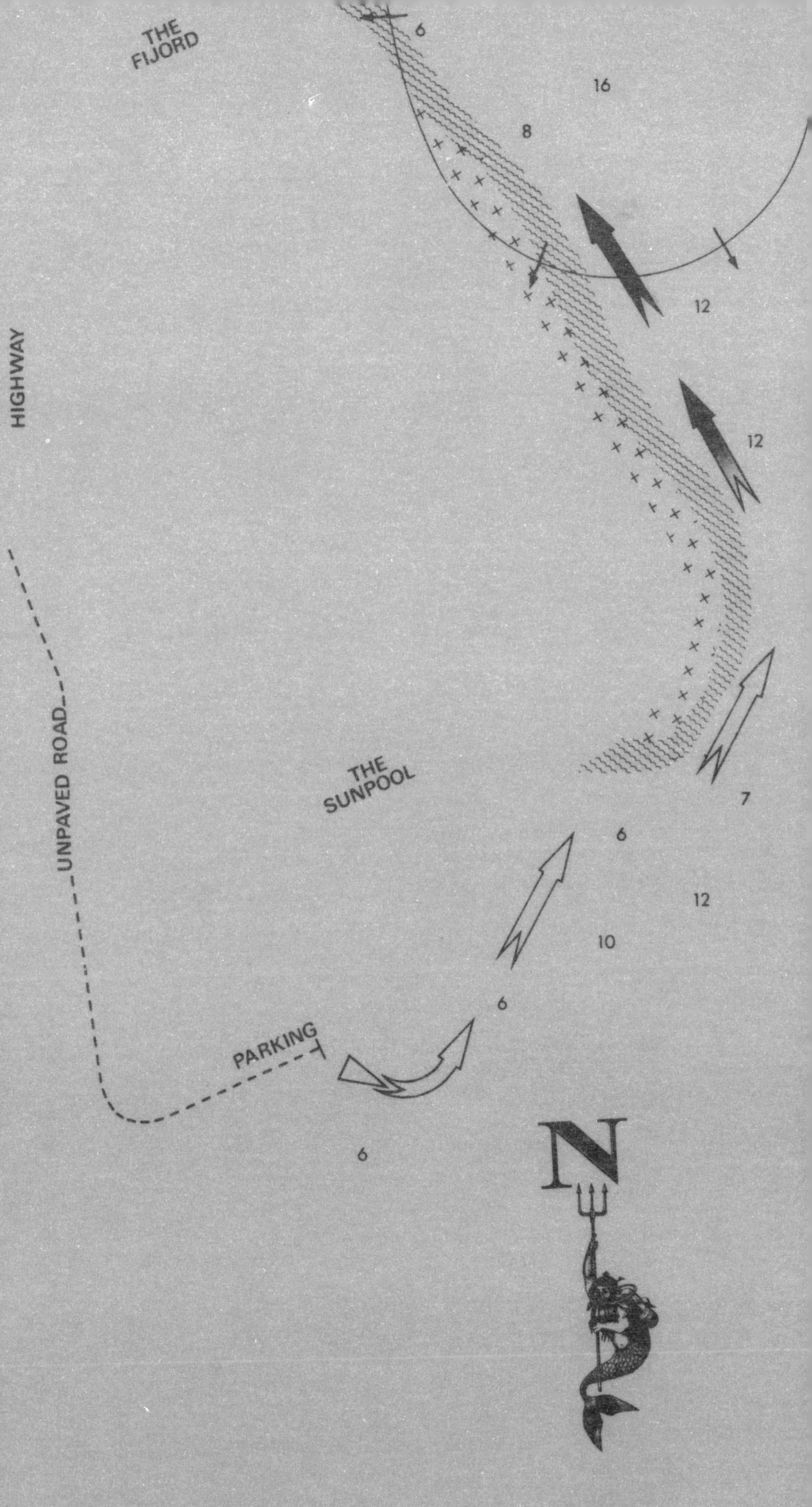
THE FIJORD
HIGHWAY
UNPAVED ROAD
THE SUNPOOL
PARKING
N
6
16
8
12
12
7
6
12
10
6
6

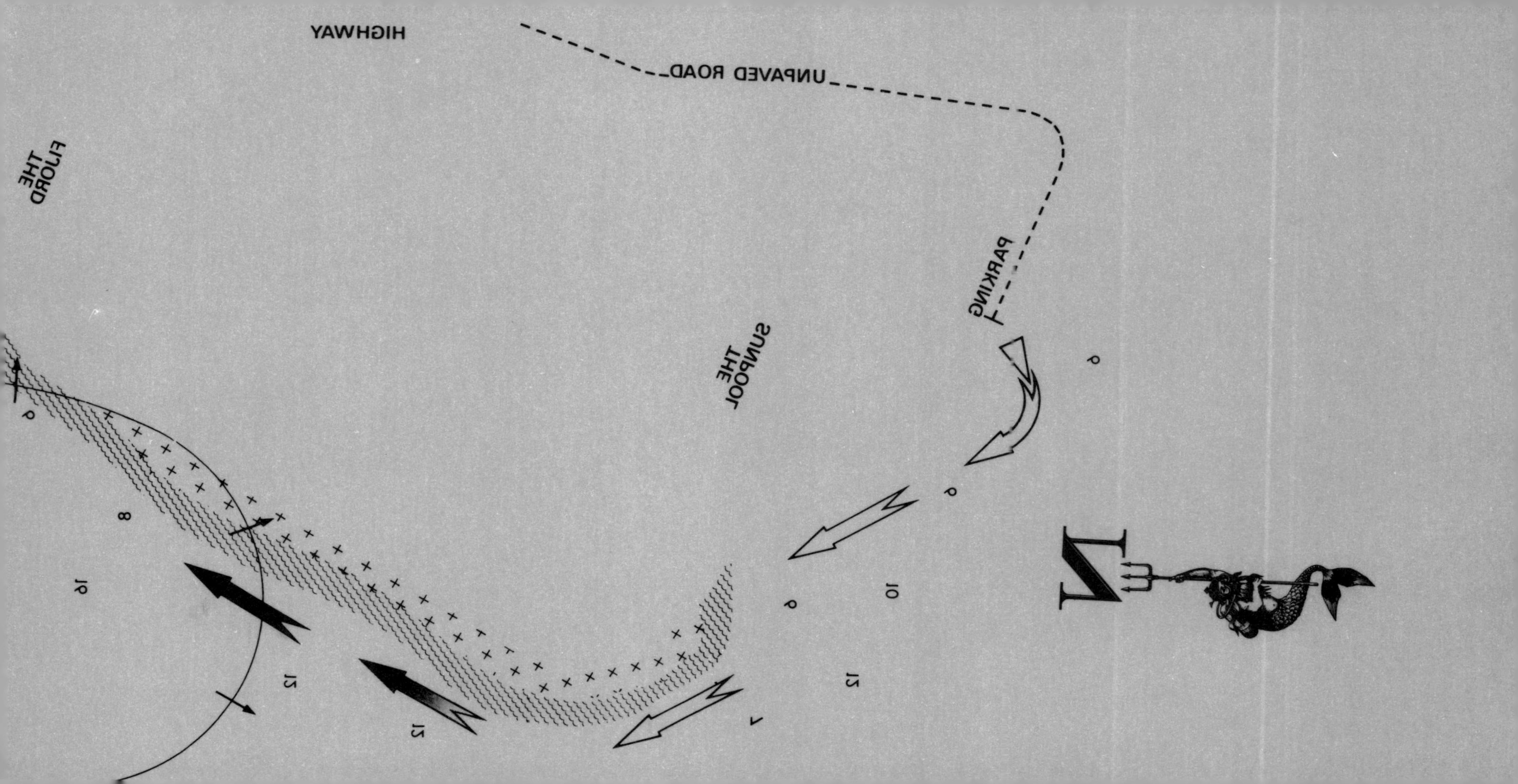
HIGHWAY
UNPAVED ROAD
PARKING
THE SUNPOOL
THE FIJORD
6
6
6
6
10
12
7
12
12
8
16
6

MARSA EL MUQABILA

Route No. 7
Ref: 12908654
34°47′20″E 29°22′00″N
Departure: Coral Beach – 26 km. (16.1 mi.)
Road Condition & Route: South on the road to Ophira with good asphalt.

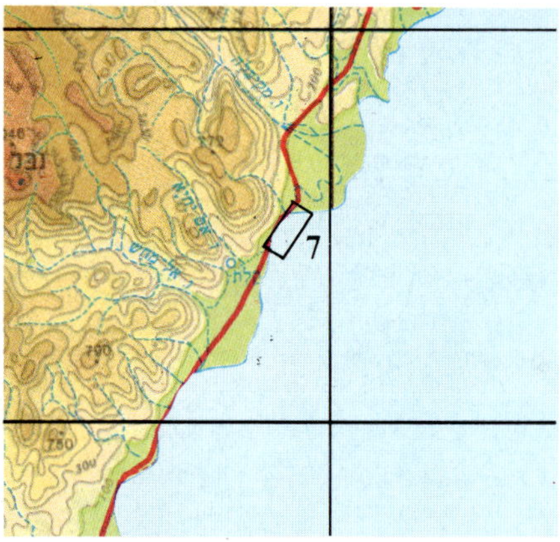

After an inland stretch of highway, you arrive at your diving site 26 kilometers from Coral Beach as the highway returns to the sea. You will see a wide and deep bay about 1 km. (0.62 mi.) long: one of the richest and most exciting dives in the Eilat area.

The road runs next to the bay protected from the rare south storms by a stone enbankment (A). A narrow reef runs parallel to the enbankment beginning at the north end of the bay. Park your vehicle and begin your dive there. Don't try to struggle over the enbankment. As you fin south along the reef you will see a gently descending sandy slope. It fills in completely with coral and coral knolls as it descends east and you will discover crevices and caves in every direction. Your best plan is to dive to the center of the bay from where you parked the vehicle, continue southwest to its southern edge and then snorkel north back to your starting point along the reef.

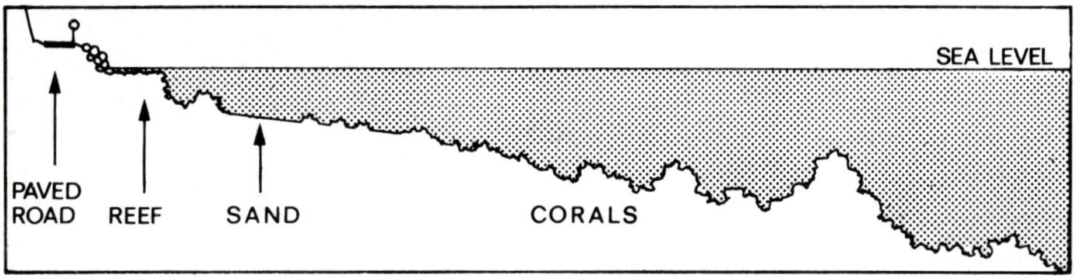

A →

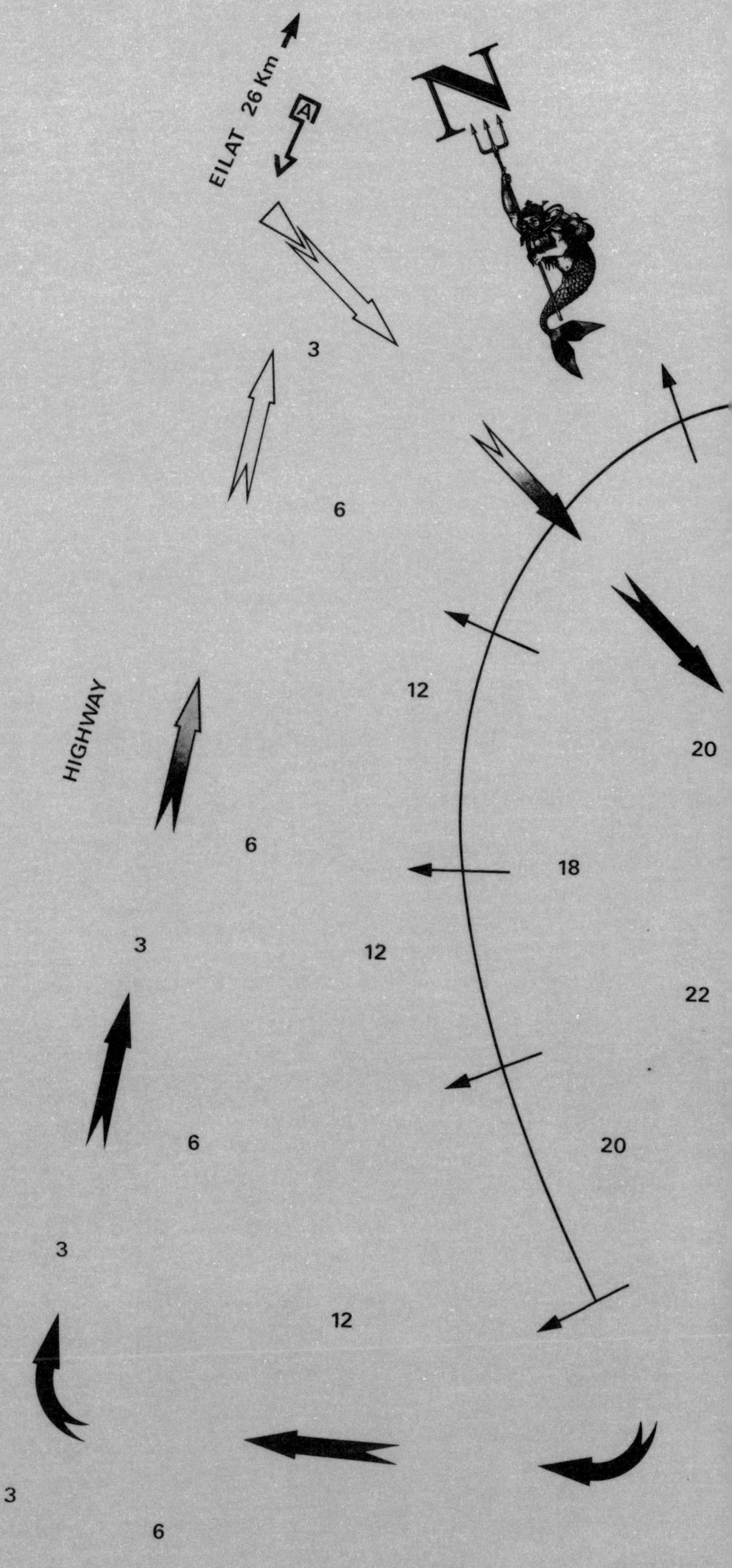
EILAT 26 Km
A
N
3
6
HIGHWAY
12
20
6
18
3
12
22
6
20
3
12
3
6

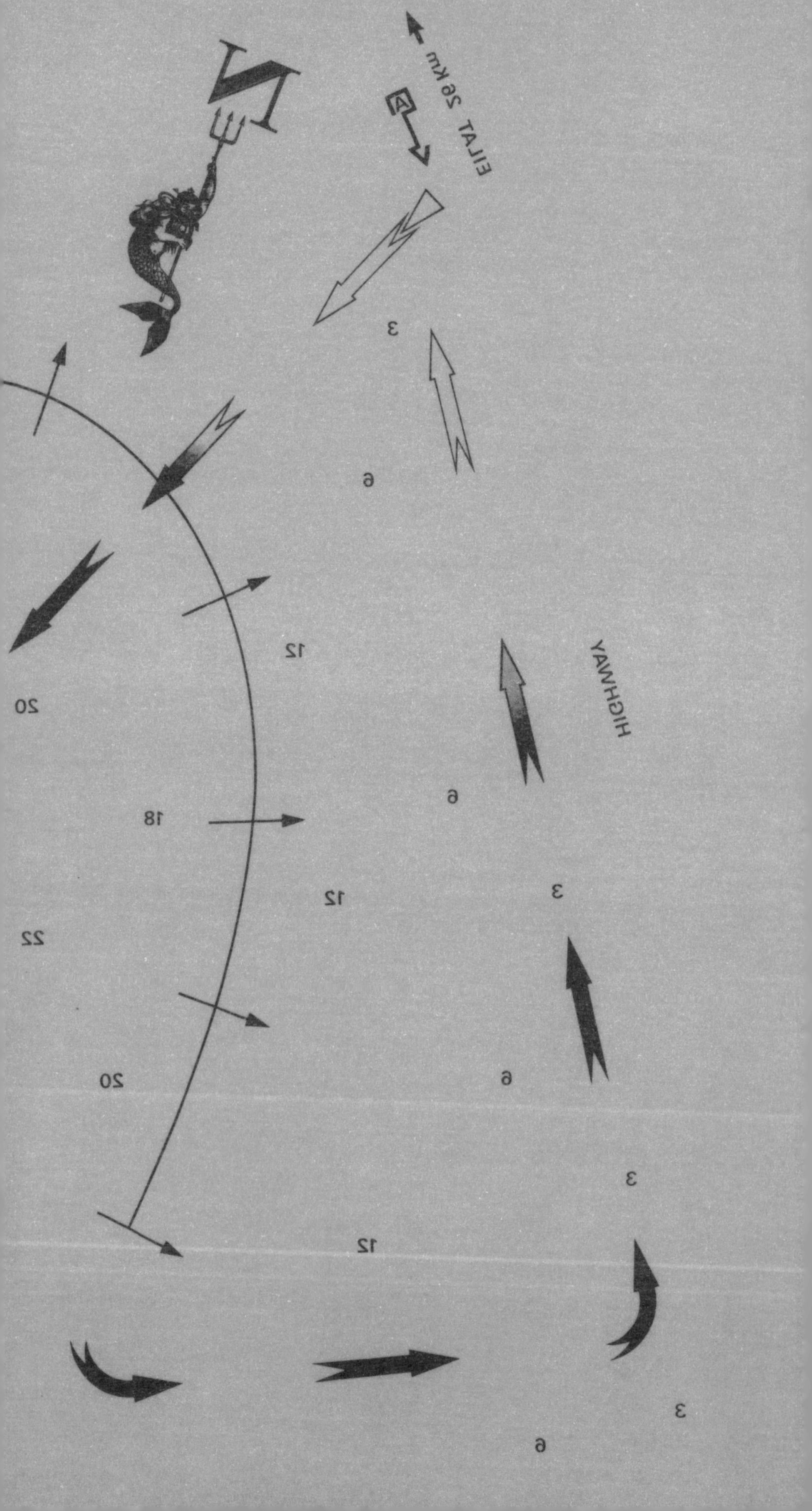
EILAT 26 km
A
HIGHWAY

RAS BURKA

Route No. 6*

Ref: 12418480 34°44′15″E 29°13′00″N
Departure: **Coral Beach** – 50 km. (31 mi.)
Road Condition & Route: South on the road to Ophira with good asphalt followed by 1 km. (0.62 mi.) of unpaved road.

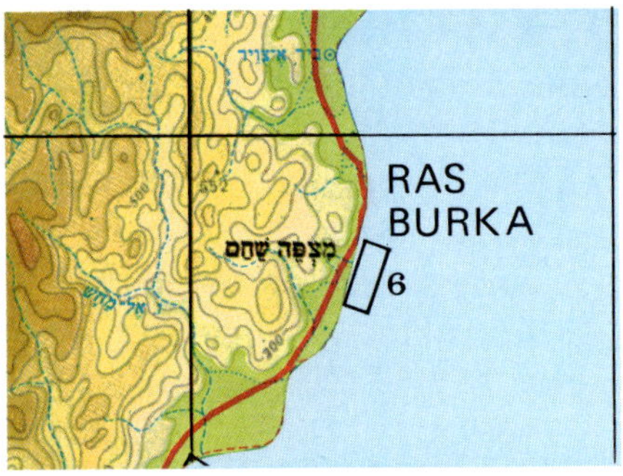

Ras Burka is the Arabic name for a prominent head in the Gulf distinguished easily by its white slope of sand. In Arabic Burka means "veil" and the head looks much like a veiled face (A). There is a small parking area on the inland side of the head next to the main highway with steps to an observation platform on top. You can study the reef below and also the Gulf for vast distances both north and south.

The reef circles the point running parallel to the shore. Drive 2 km. (1.3 mi.) south of the parking area and turn left on to the unpaved track leading to the south cove. It goes to the shore but don't take your vehicle all the way to the sea unless it has four-wheel drive. Enter the sea at this location and dive north along the coral.

A

B

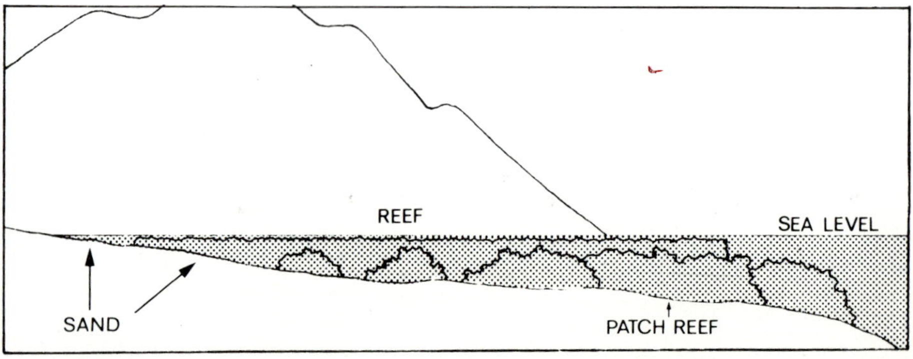

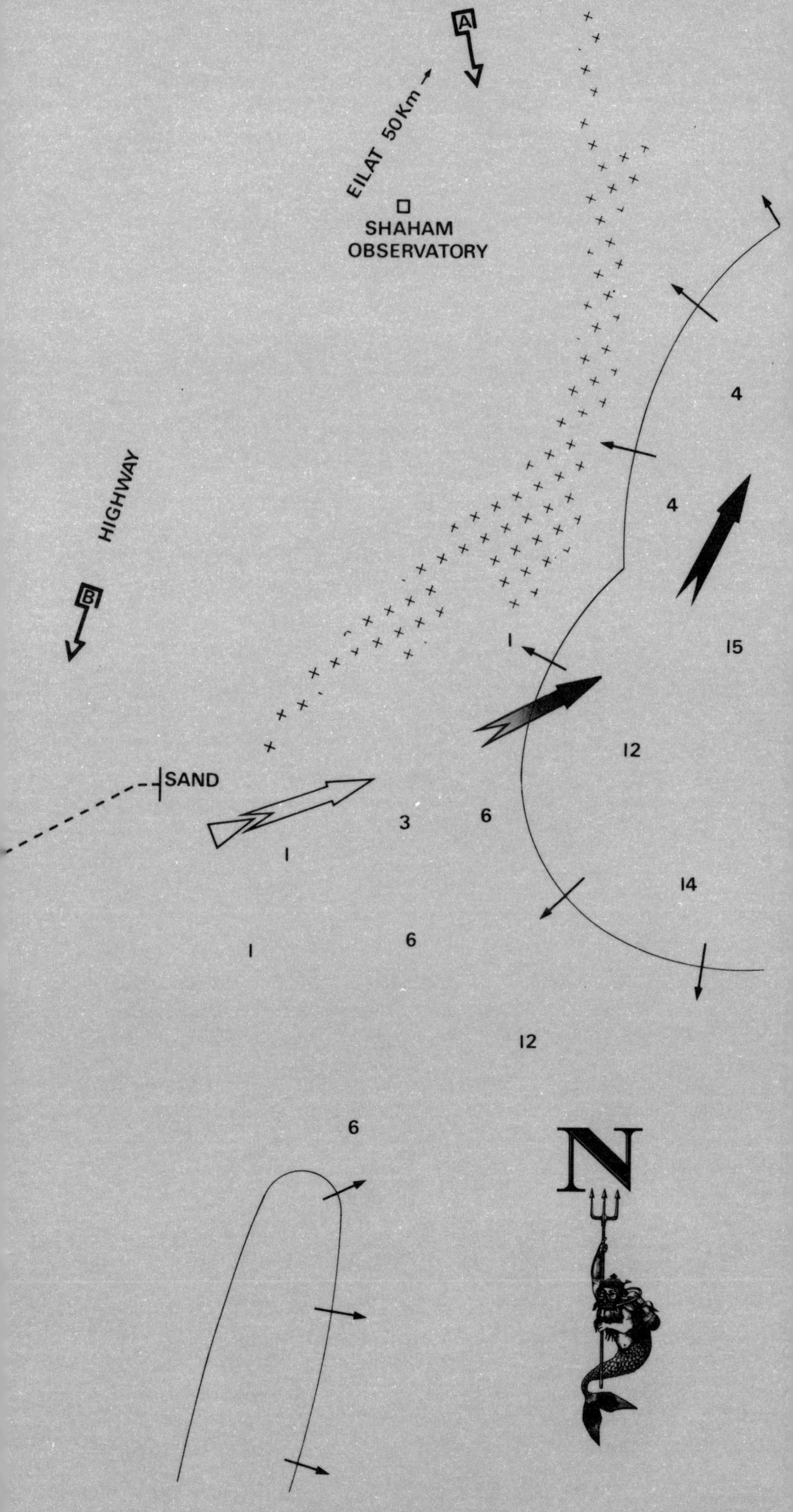

A
EILAT 50 Km →
SHAHAM OBSERVATORY
HIGHWAY
B
SAND
4
4
15
1
12
3
6
1
14
1
6
12
6
N

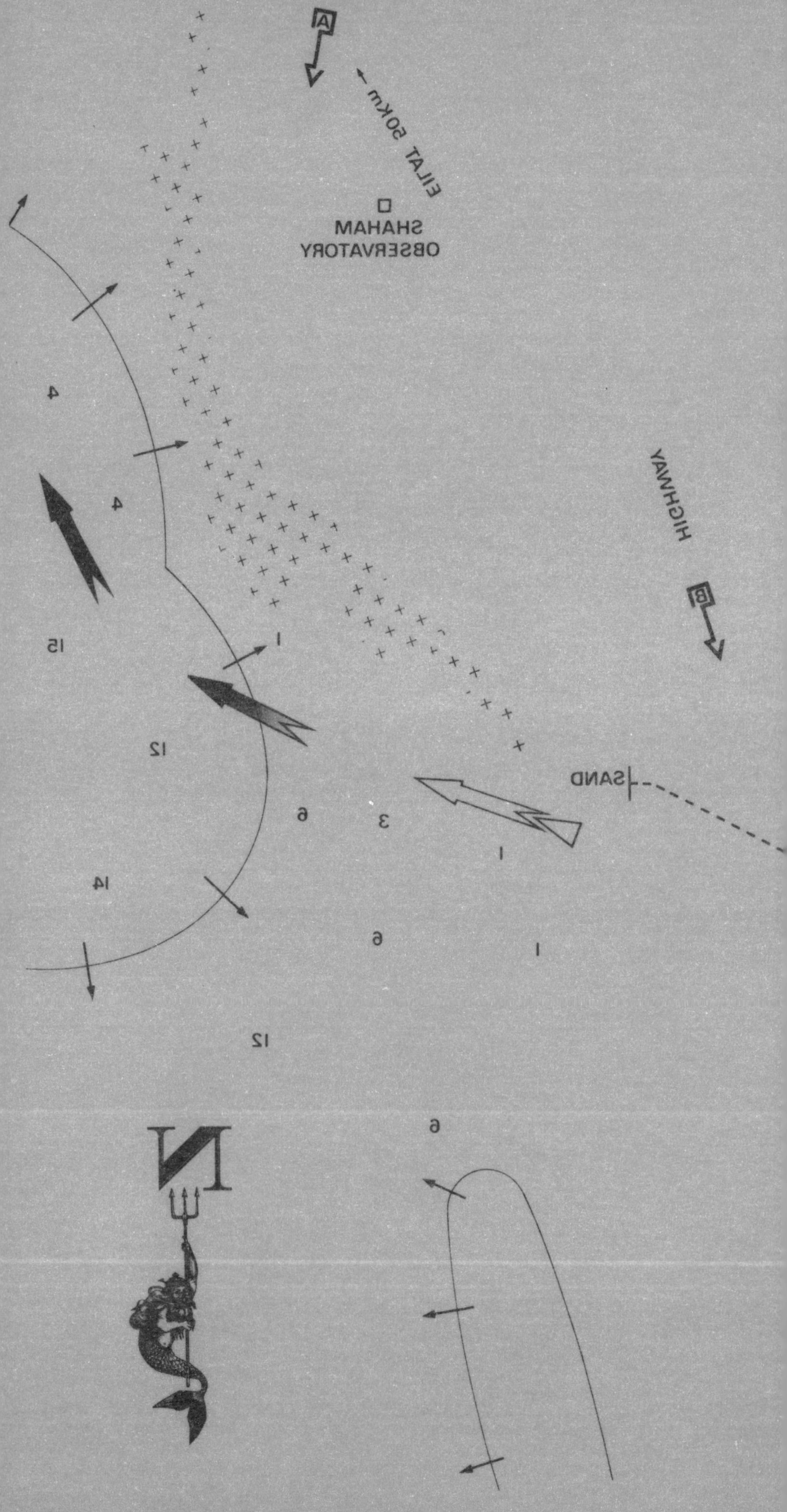

EILAT 50Km
SHAHAM OBSERVATORY
HIGHWAY
SAND
A
B
N

DAHAB

The Gulf coastline is broken by innumerable Wadi fans marching into the sea after a long journey from the Sinai highlands. A quick glance at your map shows how two of them grew to become large deltas: Nuweiba and Dahab. Wadi Dahab, as the sole outlet for a vast drainage system fed by countless tributaries, carries tons of geological debris to the sea during the rare desert flash-floods. After untold centuries of almost imperceptable invasion a great land mass, also called "Dahab", still continues its patient progress into the ocean. The fan of this delta is wide, relatively flat with a gentle slope, and encircled by mountains. The Arabic name of Dahab not only designates the Wadi and its alluvial table but an oasis. The Oasis of Dahab has, in fact, not one but three potential sources of potable water. You can locate each separate site easily by looking for three stands of palm trees to be seen near the shore in the northern, central and southern sectors of the delta.

This is Muzeini territory: a Beduin tribe building their huts, not tents, of palm leaf and stone among the trees near their wells. Looking east across the sea at Saudia Arabia about 28 km. (18 mi.) away you are standing at the widest part of the Gulf.

To find the southern oasis look southwest beyond the holiday camp and you will discover a group of palms immediately followed by mountains descending to the shoreline and terminating the delta. The central oasis circumvents a small but deep cove with a lighthouse at its northern edge. You can drive to the palm-thatched huts there and rent one from the Beduin. You can also find a coffee house among the huts to enjoy an authentic cup of Beduin coffe or soft drinks. (Obtain your water for camping, however, at Dizahav.) The northern oasis (about a kilometer — 0.6 mi. — north of the lighthouse) is the largest with much vegetation, many wells and a substantial village. As you continue north from this habitation the beach narrows and the Sinai Mts. advance toward the shore until they touch the sea at Nakab Shaheen: where both the road and the delta ends.

DISTANCES

CORAL BEACH – DAHAB JCT.	135 km. (85 mi.)
OPHIRA – DAHAB JCT.	95 km. (60 mi.)
DAHAB JCT. – DIZAHAV	6 km. (3.8 mi.)
DIZAHAV – CENTRAL OASIS (LIGHTHOUSE)	3 km. (1.9 mi.)
NORTHERN OASIS – THE CANYON	5 km. (3.2 mi.)
NORTHERN OASIS – NAKAB SHAHEEN	7.2 km. (4.5 mi.)
DIZAHAV – SOUTHERN OASIS	7.2 km. (4.5 mi.)

SOUTHERN OASIS

Route No. 9

Ref.: 09627618
34°27′00″E 28°26′30″N
Departure: Dizahav – 7.2 km (4.5 mi.)
Road Condition & Route: South along the shore on a passable but difficult unpaved road.

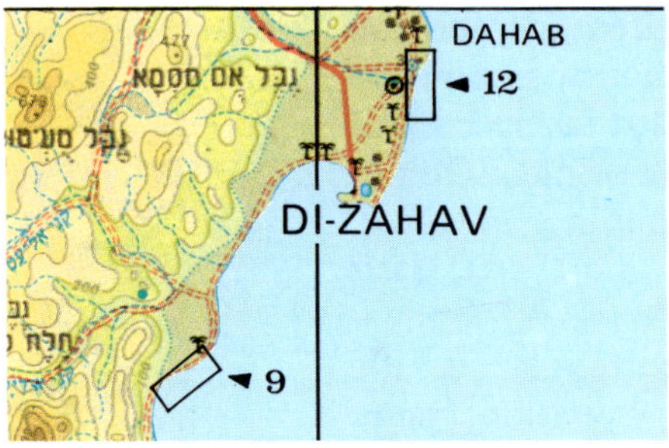

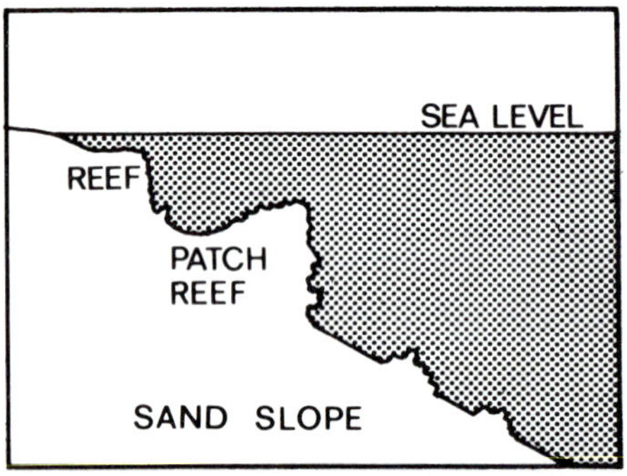

Turn left onto a dirt road about 100 m. (330 ft.) after departing from Dizahav on the asphalt leading to Dahab Junction. The rough track leading to the southern oasis runs close behind the holiday camp and then turns south towards those palm trees clearly in view about 7 km. (4.4 mi.) away. This oasis is excellent for camping and for its aura of quiet tranquility. (Remember, however, to take your water from Dizahav.)

The reef table at this site is quite narrow, about 10 m. (33 ft.) wide, and the coral ends at 3–6 m. (10–20 ft.) depth. Directly from the reef, however, a steep sandy slope quickly descends to 35 m. (115 ft.) and more. The slope supports numerous coral knolls and patches. The road ends with the delta where the mountains reach the sea beyond the oasis. If you want to explore the reefs there, a boat is recommended.

Special Note: If your water runs out and you must use a Beduin well, boil the water or use purification tablets. Otherwise, you might miss a good dive because of diarrhea.

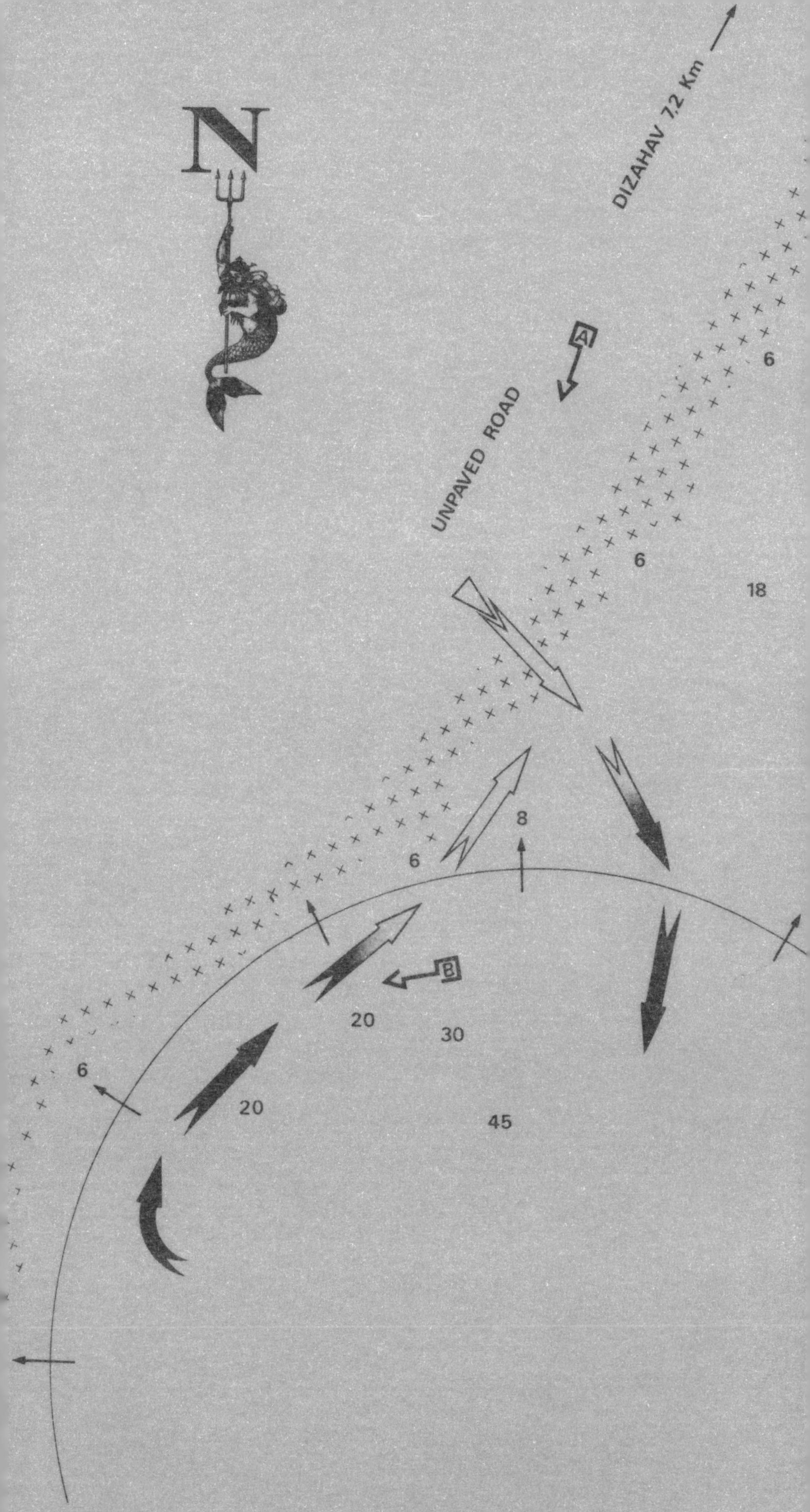
N
DIZAHAV 7,2 Km
UNPAVED ROAD
A
B
6
6
18
8
6
20
30
6
20
45

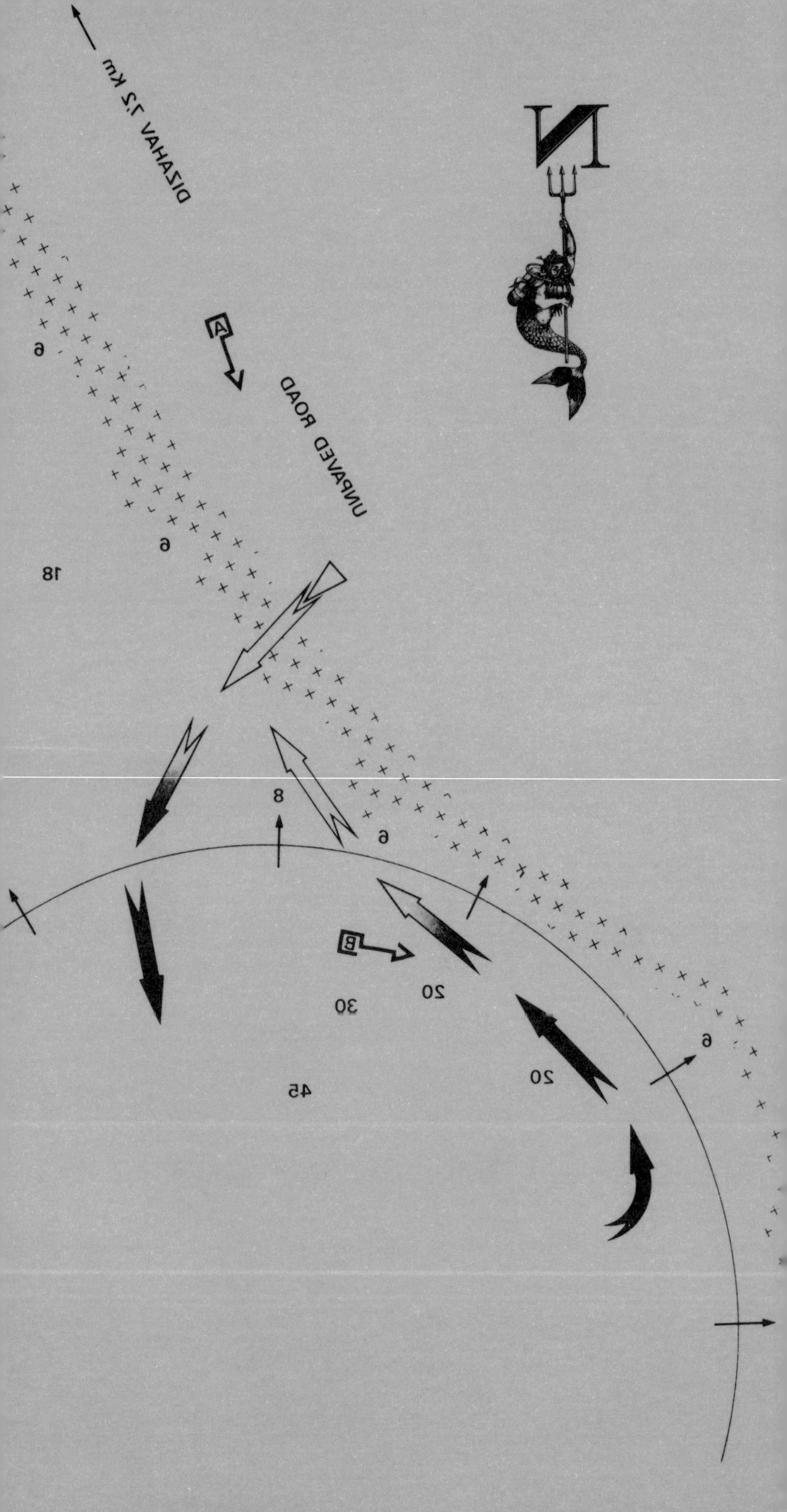
DIZAHAV 1.2 Km
UNPAVED ROAD
N
A
B
6
6
18
8
6
20
30
20
6
45

THE LIGHTHOUSE

Route No. 12

Ref: 10227688
34°30′30″E 28°30′00″N

Departure: Dizahav – 3 km. (1.9 mi.)
Road Condition & Route: East to the shore on unpaved road.

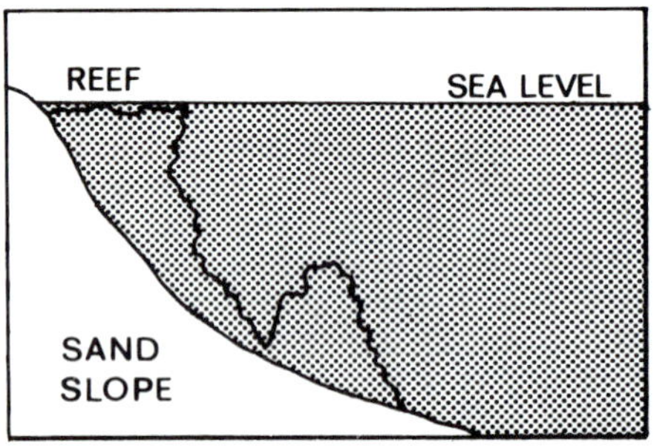

Most divers try their luck at **The Canyon** first so you will probably be familiar with the central oasis and its lighthouse. A few hundred meters after leaving the Dizahav holiday camp and driving toward Dahab Junction, you will discover an unpaved road heading east to the central oasis. At the end of this dirt road make a 90° turn left (north). (Do not turn left onto any one of the several Beduin tracks appearing before the road ends.) Continue north about 300 m. (1,000 ft.) until you find yourself opposite the lighthouse (A). There are a few Beduin huts scattered around the lighthouse tower, available for rental, and a vehicle can be driven into the area.

Enter the sea due south of the lighthouse. Dive down the steep sandy slope and then turn east to find the seaward wall of the reef table. The reef will curve parallel with the shore until you are finning north. This is a magnificent formation with a vertical wall ending at 30–40 m. (100–130 ft.) depth and teeming with flora and fauna (B). There are also a few gigantic coral patches off the reef on sandy bottom.

Special Note: There is a strong prevailing north wind on the Dahab delta and you will usually encounter both breakers and a strong surface current if you attempt diving entry due east of the lighthouse. Follow your guide and do it the easy way.

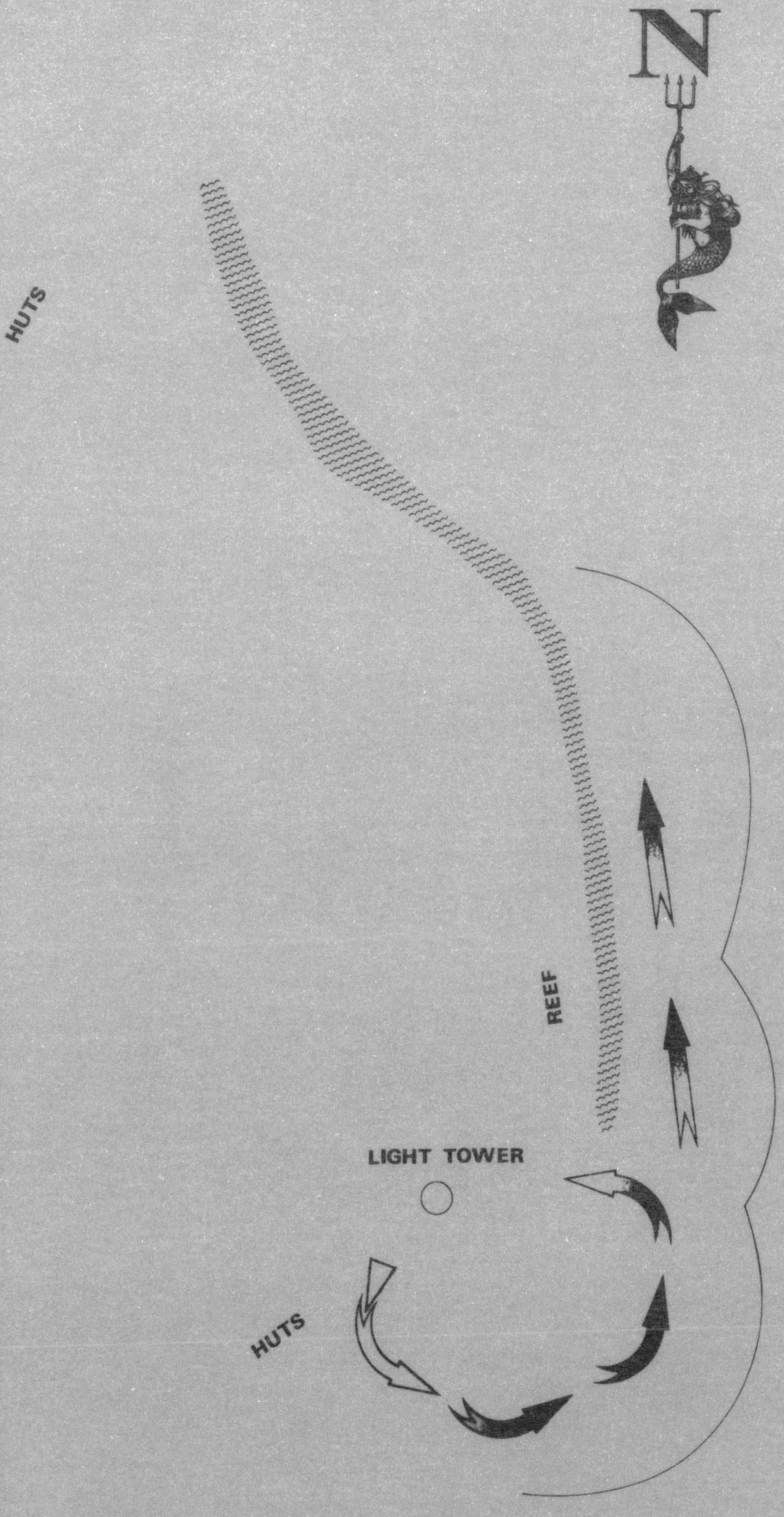
N
HUTS
REEF
LIGHT TOWER
HUTS

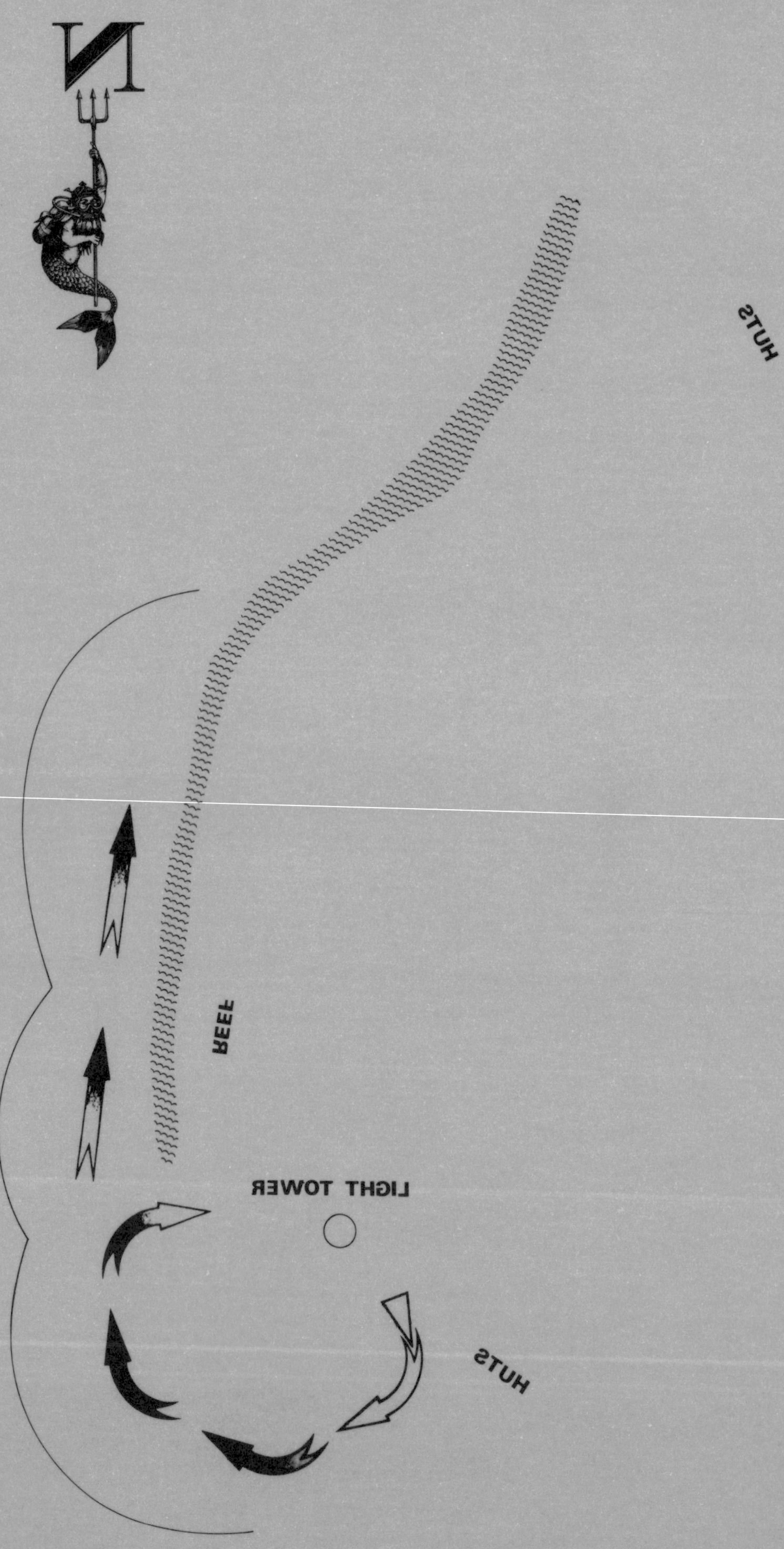
N
REEF
LIGHT TOWER
HUTS
HUTS

NAKAB SHAHEEN

Route No. 11 Ref: 10467772
34°32′00″E 28°34′45″N
Departure: Dizahav – 11.2 km. (7 mi.)
Road Condition & Route: North along the shore via unpaved road becoming impassable without four-wheel drive about 200 m. (660 ft.) before the site.

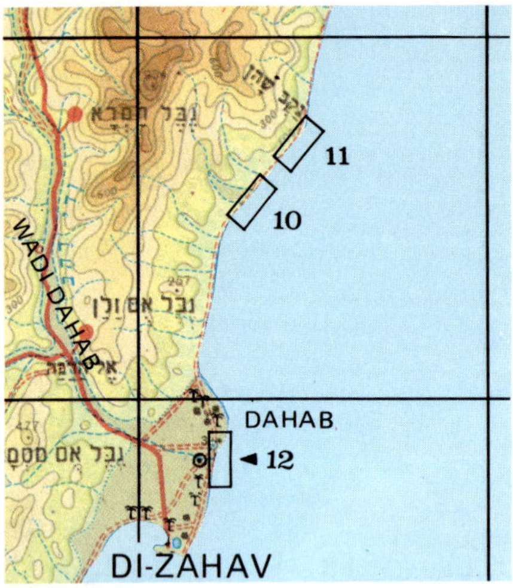

A

B

Nakab Shaheen ("Hook Pass" in Arabic) is a high and narrow pass at the northern end of the delta. The area of your dive has topography similar to that found at Ras Muhammed with high bluffs composed of fossil coral dropping straight to the sea.

However, the most interesting phenomenon on this stretch of shore is the enormous hole in the reef table plunging to depths far beyond the diver's range. The site is exactly 2.2 km. (1.4 mi.) north of **The Canyon.** Just continue along the coast road until you reach an abrupt, steep grade. You need four-wheel drive to advance up this hill. With a standard vehicle, park at this point and unpack your gear. Enter the sea and cross easily over the narrow reef table. Snorkel north past the high and sheer bluff until you reach the seaward entrance to the hole.

If you can climb to the summit of this grade with a stronger vehicle, the hole will be seen directly ahead about 200 m. (660 ft.) further on. Drive up to its edge and begin the dive from there. The road terminates a short distance beyond this point.

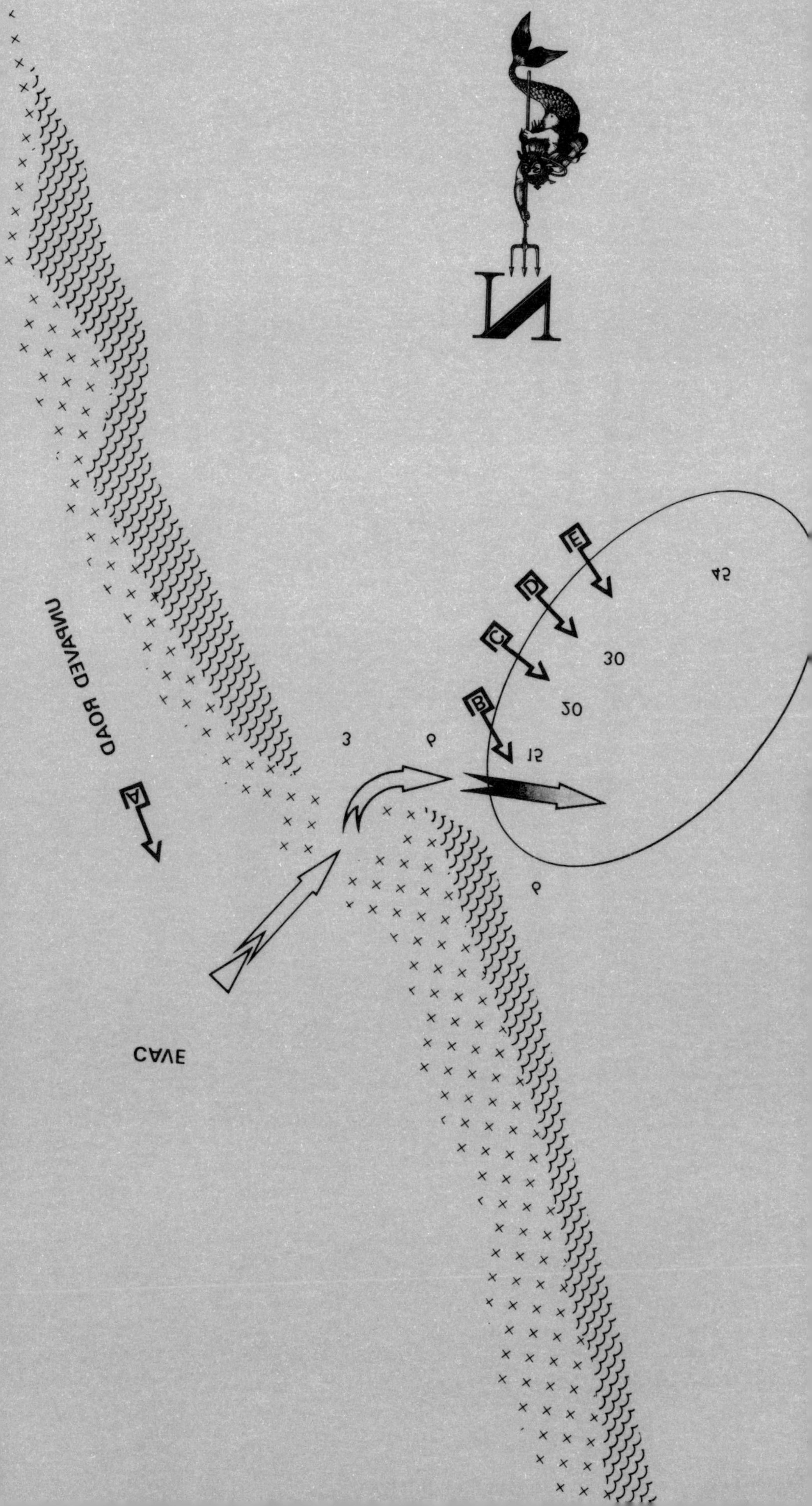

N
CAVE
UNPAVED ROAD
A
B
C
D
E
3
6
6
15
20
30
45

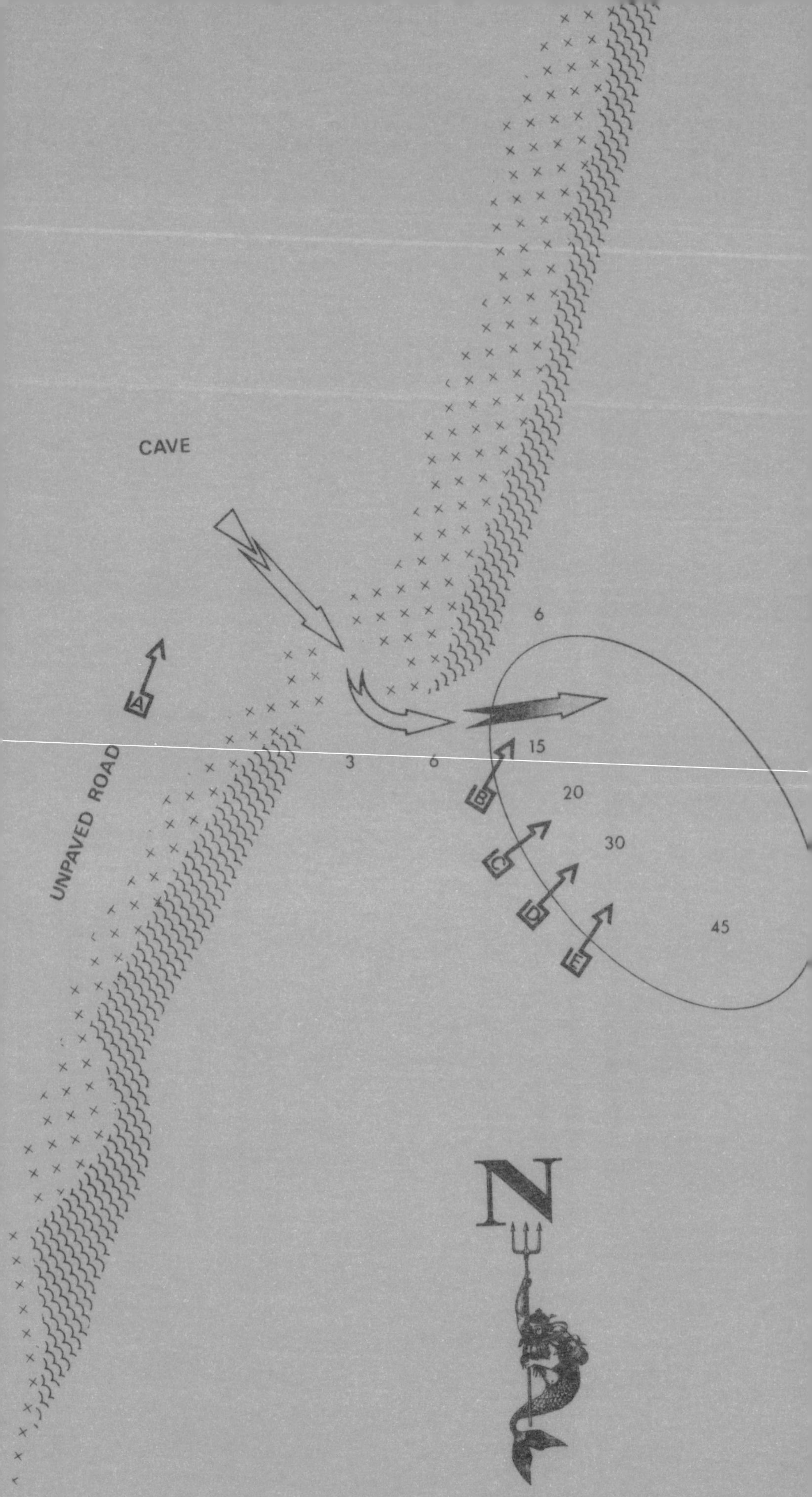
CAVE
A
UNPAVED ROAD
3
6
6
15
20
30
45
B
C
D
E
N

THE CANYON

Route No. 10
Ref: 10307732
34°31′15″E 28°34′00″N
Departure: Dizahav – 9 km. (5.7 mi.)
Road Condition & Route: North along the delta shore on unpaved road.

A fantastic dive because of its location, depth, and beauty: the canyon is a diver's delight not to be missed. It can easily be missed, however, unless you follow instructions carefully.

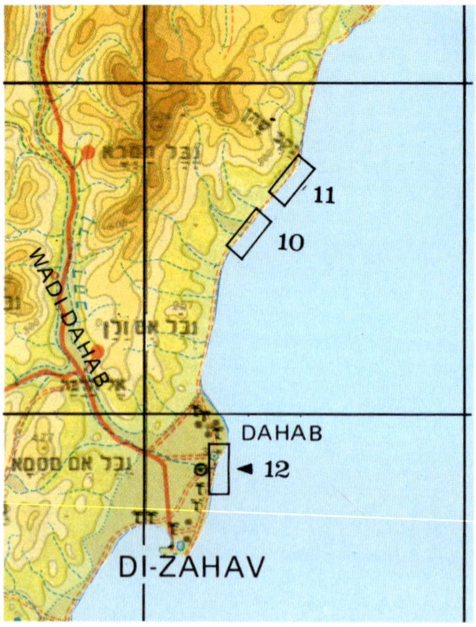

A few hundred meters after leaving the Dizahav holiday camp and driving toward Dahab Junction, you will discover an unpaved road heading east to the central oasis (**The Lighthouse**). At the end of this dirt road make a 90° turn left (north) and continue to the northern end of the delta. (If you mistakenly turn left onto one of the several Beduin tracks before the road ends, don't stop or backtrack but continue; they all lead to the northern oasis and the canyon is beyond it.) As you drive about 800 m. (0.5 mi.) beyond the northern oasis, where the mountains reach the sea and the road is along the shore, drive carefully because the way is narrow and difficult. Continuing along the coast 5 km. (3.1 mi.) from the northern oasis you will approach a cliff with a cave on its southern wall (A). Look to the sea a few meters before reaching this cliff and you will sight a lagoon with a break through the reef.

The reef itself runs parallel to the shore with 6–8 m. (20–27 ft.) depth and a sandy slope descends from the bottom of its seaward wall. The slope gradually fills in completely with coral before levelling-off at 50–60 m. (165–198 ft.) depth. The canyon begins near the reef and ends at the bottom of the slope. Caution: this site is so incredibly beautiful, so fascinating, and so deep, you are advised to plan very carefully. Do not continue your exploration to the end of the canyon without rechecking your dive plan, air, depth, and decompression.

Enter the sea via the lagoon and do not attempt to cross over the reef table. Snorkel through the reef via the break in the lagoon and then turn immediately left (north) finning parallel to the seaward wall.

A →

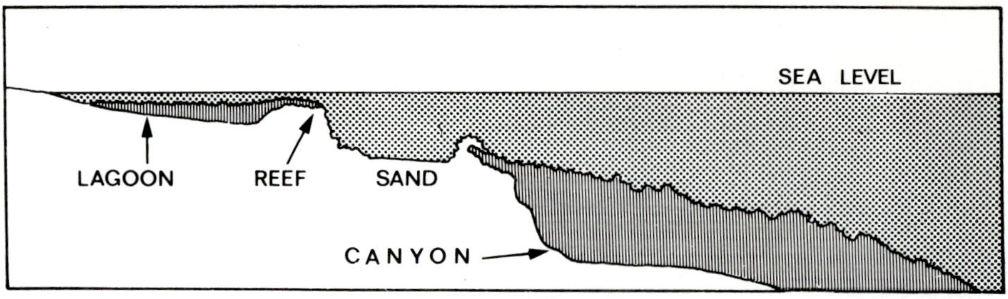

When you have snorkeld along the reef to a point exactly opposite the cliff (A) turn right (east) and you will see a large isolated underwater rock split by a crevice (B). (It is alone and can't be missed.) That crevice marks the beginning of the canyon. Dive to the bottom but do not enter the crevice at this point. Just follow it and a major opening will appear where you can enter and begin your exploration. Caution: again check your dive plan. The canyon is winding between vertical walls on its sandy bottom but sometimes it is very narrow above and sometimes wide enough to make an exit. Do not continue to the end without exact knowledge of your air-supply, decompression needs, and surface weather conditions. It is easy to be distracted by the splendor of this marinescape and find yourself at 40 m. (130 ft.) without sufficient air.

Special Note: When the sea is rough and a strong north wind is blowing, avoid snorkeling too near or over the reef table and dive through the break to enter and exit from the lagoon.

B

C

D

E

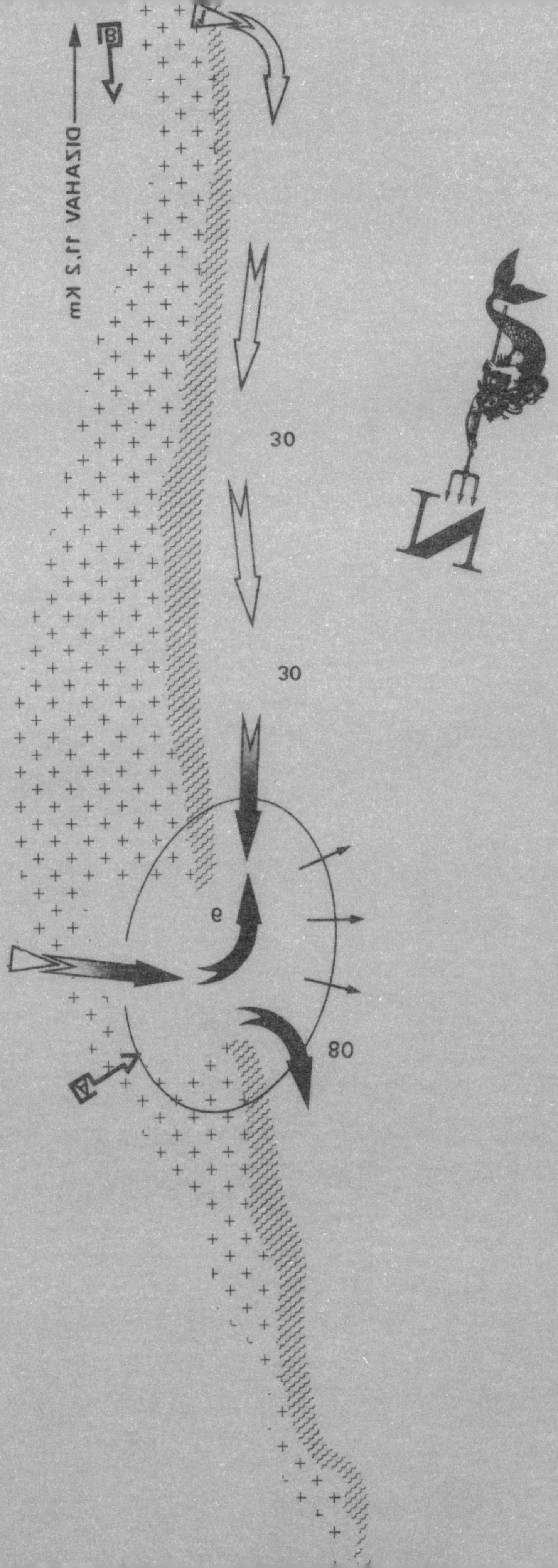

DIZAHAV 11.2 Km
B
30
30
A
80
N

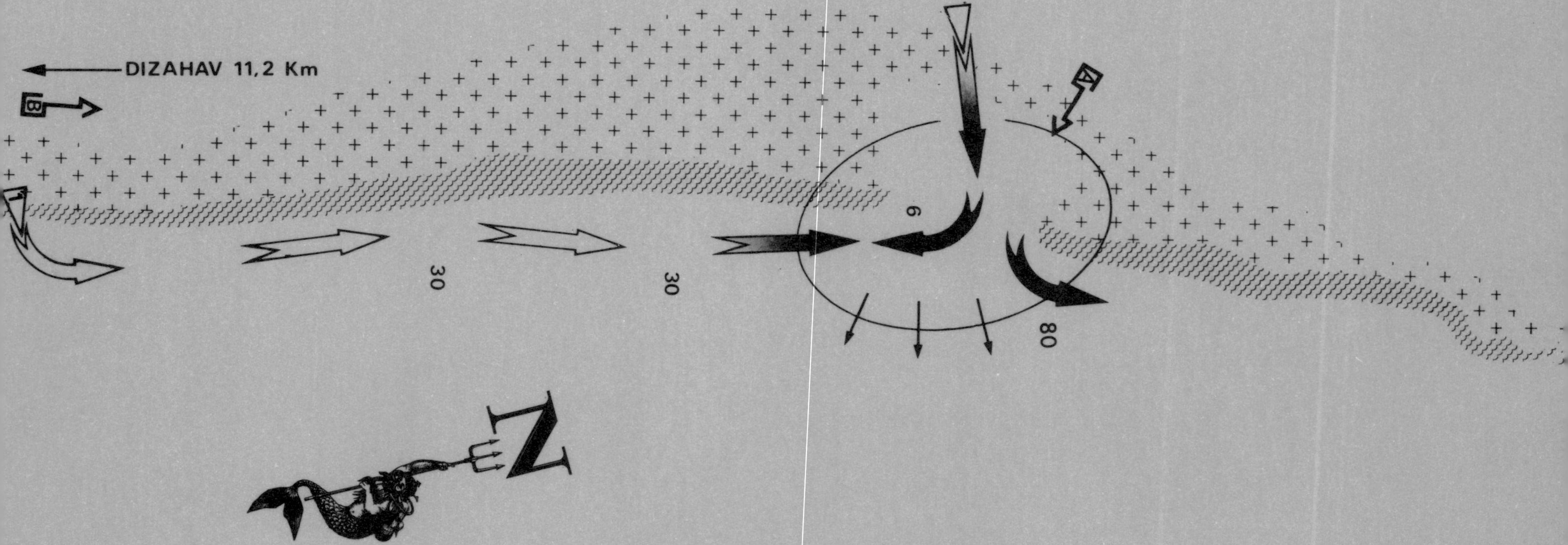
DIZAHAV 11,2 Km
B
1
30
30
9
80
A
N

NABEK

Nabek is an oasis resting on the shore of a wide delta stretching 5–7 km. (3–4.5 mi.) from the mountains to the sea. This long delta is also fed by several Wadis of which Wadi Kid is the major contributor. Among the few oases on this stretch of coast, the one called Nabek may be distinguished only by the fact that it is the southernmost watering spot on the Gulf coast. When compared with those at Dahab, they are only a few clumps of solitary palms. The water is very saline but potable enough for survival. Bring your own water to the area, however, and don't rely upon the oases. Consistent with the stature of these oases, the delta is only sparsely populated by a few Beduin families.

The fan at Nabek ends in the north where the mountains return to shore and you can not reach Dahab by driving north along the coast. The southern edge ends at Ras Nasrani where the coastal terrain begins a marked transformation.

There is a good asphalt road from Ophira Junction running northeast past the airfield to Ras Nasrani. The parking area near the end of this road faces the Straits and Island of Tiran: entrance to the Gulf of Eilat. From Ras Nasrani north to Nabek you will be driving on unpaved but usually well-graded road. Warning: although the mine fields in this area are well marked and fenced, do not leave the road while still in their vicinity. About 4.5 km. (2.8 mi.) north of Ras Nasrani, as the road runs inland but parallel to the Gulf, you will see a grounded ship, the *Yael Daroma,* sitting high on the reef table. When the road reaches the shore at Nabek drive 4 km. (2.5 mi.) further north to a beautiful lagoon surrounded by mangroves. This northern lagoon is the best site for camping with shelters on the beach built of palm logs and thatched with their leaves. If you are planning a few days' diving in the area set up headquarters here and journey north by vehicle to the various sites.

You can also reach Nabek from the north. An unpaved road through Wadi Kid branches off from the main Eilat-Ophira highway 54 km. (34 mi.) south from the Dahab Junction. A Beduin coffee house, palm thatched, will help you identify the Wadi Kid turn-off when arriving from the north. Only coffee, soft drinks and cigarettes are available but it provides the first and last shade for many kilometers and a bit of rest before navigating Wadi Kid. Stay alert after driving east through the Wadi because you will meet a fork on the delta: you may turn south to Nabek at this point or continue east to the sea where the Wadi Kid route ends at the north-south coastal road, also unpaved (Ref: 09447336). There is a solitary palm tree at this junction with the coast road (A). North you can drive to **Shora el-Manqata** and the wreck of **The Maria Schröder.** South you will find the mangroves of **Nahalat el-tel** and, beyond, the north lagoon of Nabek.

DISTANCES

OPHIRA (PETROL STATION) – RAS NASRANI	24 km. (15 mi.)
RAS NASRANI – NORTH LAGOON AT NABEK	30.6 km. (10.3 mi.)
NORTH LAGOON – PALM TREE JCT. (REF: 09447336)	8.5 km. (5.8 mi.)
PALM TREE JCT. – EILAT-OPHIRA HIGHWAY (VIA WADI KID)	14.2 km. (9 mi.)
DAHAB JCT. – WADI KID	54 km. (34 mi.)

NAHALAT EL-TEL

Route No. 13*

Ref: 09487288
34°27′00″E 28°08′30″N
Departure: Eilat or Ophira
Road Condition & Route: See NABEK.

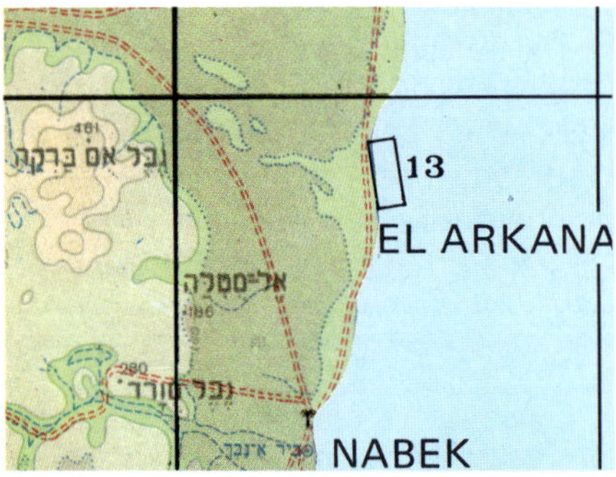

The oasis of El-Arkana is situated south of the Palm Tree Junction on a long shallow bay bordered by mangroves both north and south. Following the road north from Ras Nasrani it is exactly 15 km. (9.5 mi.) to **Nahalat el-tel**. Look for the two palm trees standing together on the sea side of the road marking exactly your diving site (A). The shallow bay with muddy bottom about 20 cm. (8 in.) deep extends to a shallow reef table about 60 m. (200 ft.) offshore. Walk to the table and begin your dive there. Snorkel across the muddy channel, with poor visibility and a depth of 6 m. (20 ft.), to reach an exciting cluster of reef knolls resting on sandy bottom in clear water. If you are in the Nabek area, don't miss a dive here. It's magnificent!

A →

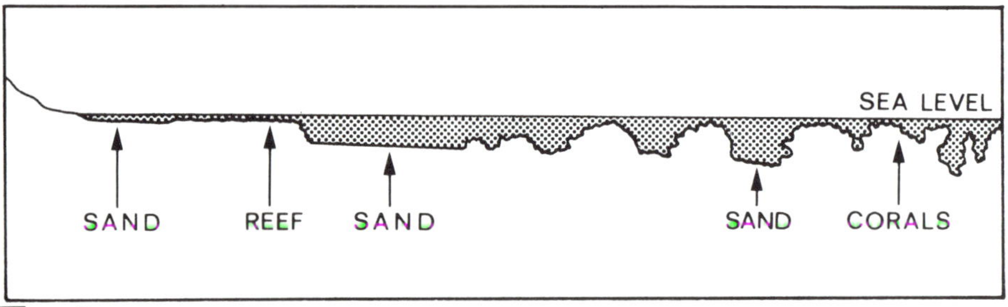

B →

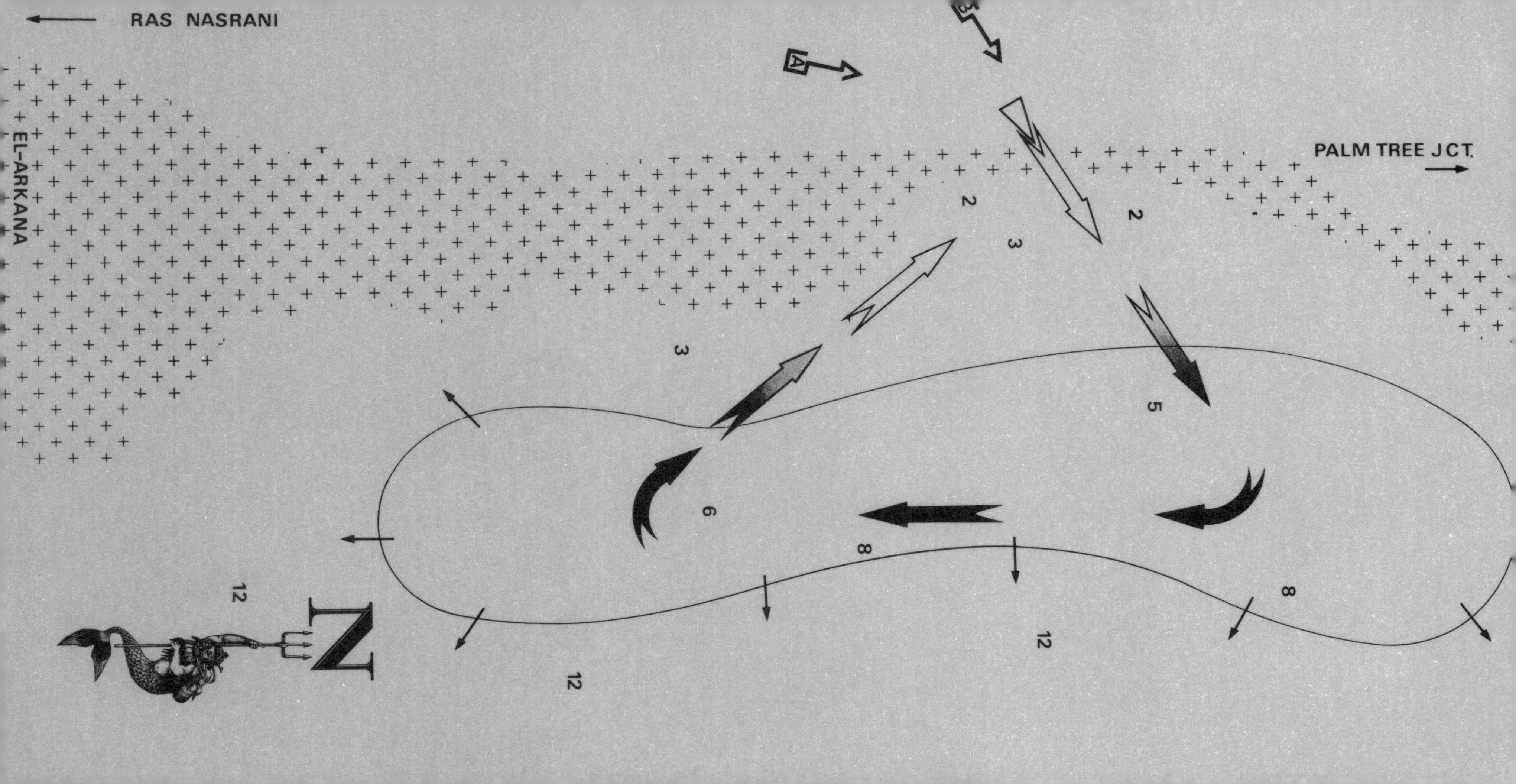
RAS NASRANI
PALM TREE JCT.
EL-ARKANA
A
B
2
2
3
3
5
6
8
8
12
12
12
12
N

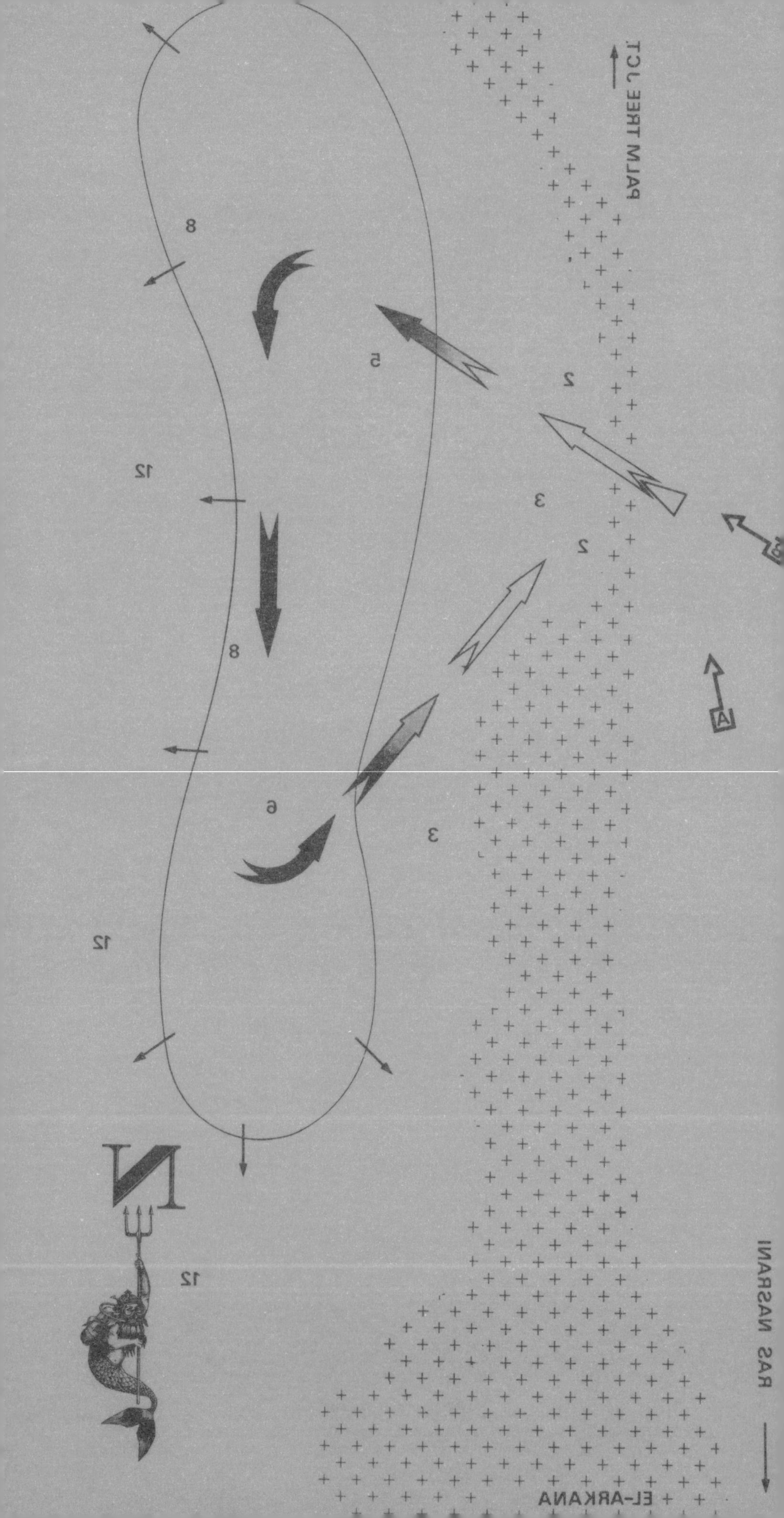

PALM TREE JCT.
RAS NASRANI
EL-ARKANA
A
B
N
2
2
3
3
5
6
8
8
12
12
12

MARIA SCHRÖDER

Route No. 14
Ref: 09527347
34°28'00"E 28°11'30"N
Departure: Eilat or Ophira
Road Condition & Route:
See NABEK

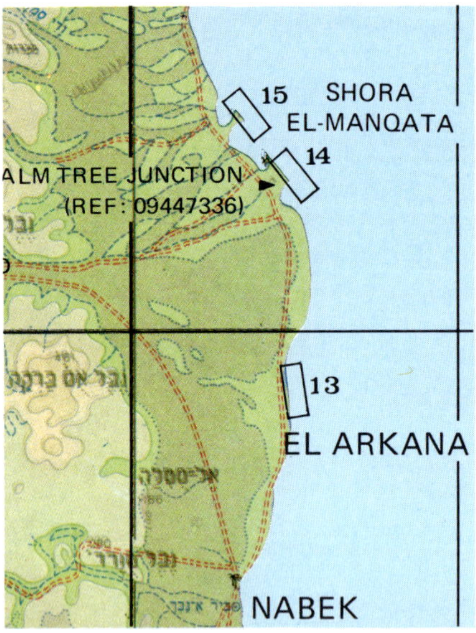

In 1965 a raging Gulf storm lifted the Maria Schröder like a baby and deposited this ship on the seaward edge of the reef table. Till today one can still see her two anchors and their chains flung far to the sea in a vain attempt to keep her off the reef (A).

The ship is north of the Palm Tree Junction and exactly 5.5 km. (3.5 mi.) north along the road from **Nahalat el-tel.** Don't try to reach the wreck through the mangroves but stop opposite the ship and then turn right to the lagoon (**D**). You can walk across the shallow and rocky lagoon almost to the ship. If you are touring with a four-wheel drive vehicle there is an alternative approach. You can approach a bit closer to the ship, only at low tide, by driving to the northern end of the lagoon.

Special Note: Under no circumstances should you enter the ocean for a dive, not from the northern end of the lagoon and not from the reef table, when there are rough seas.

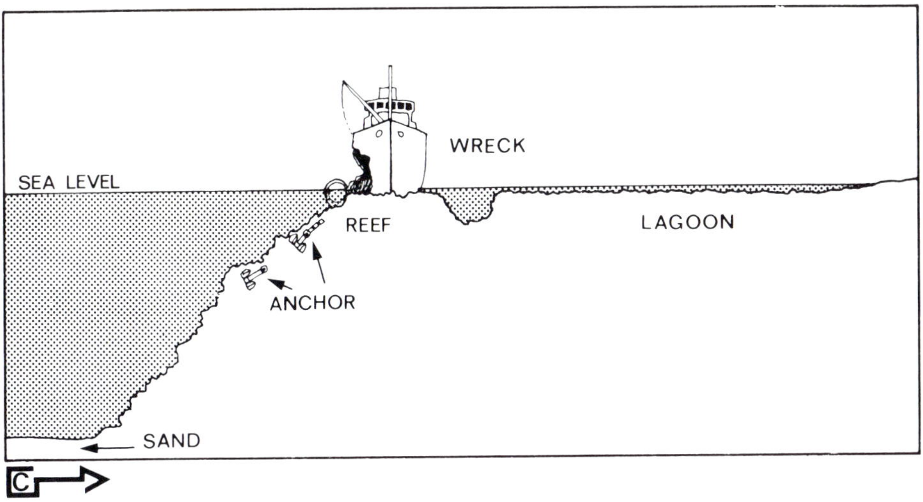
WRECK
SEA LEVEL
REEF
LAGOON
ANCHOR
SAND
C

D

E

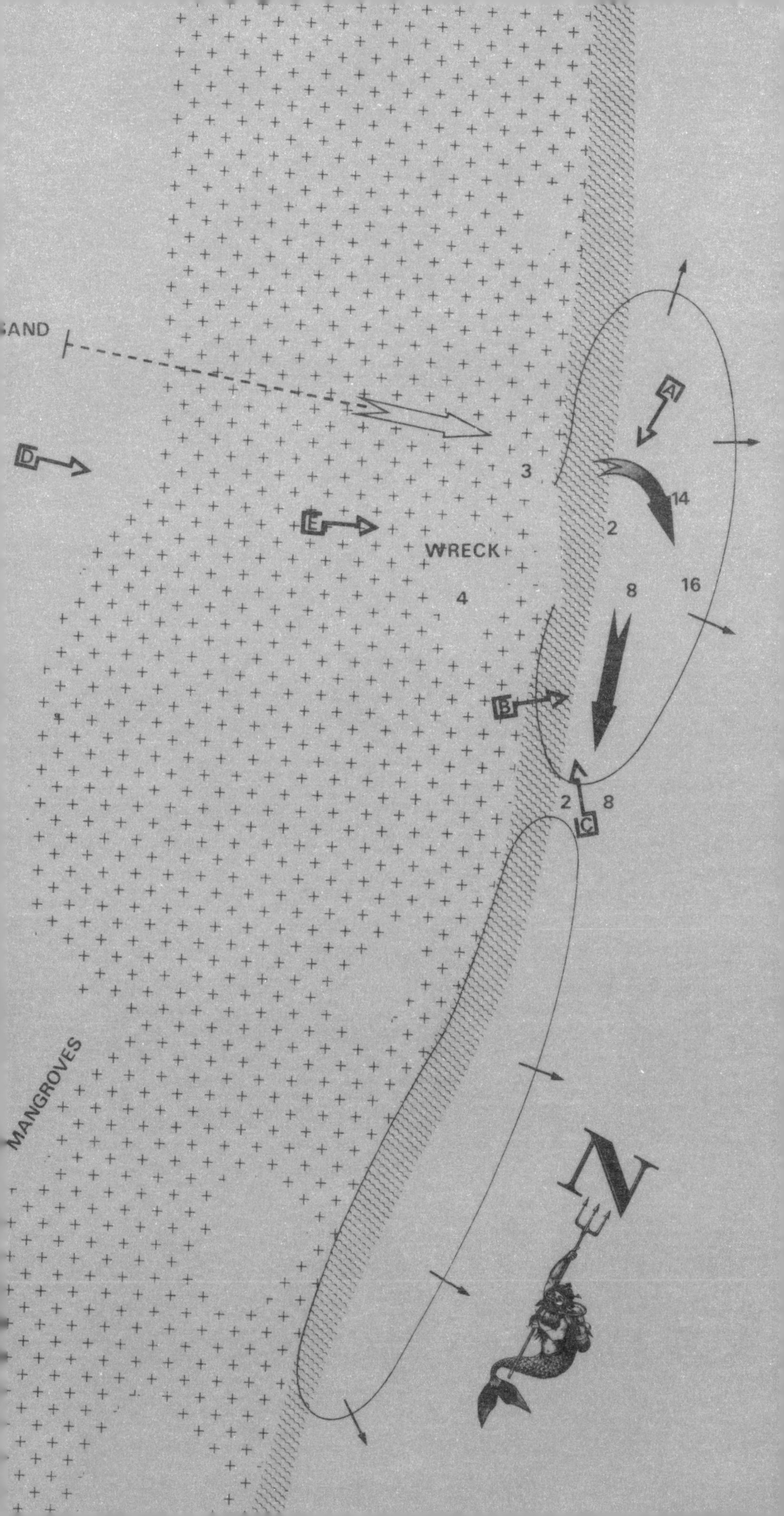
SAND
A
D
3
14
E
2
WRECK
8
16
4
B
2
8
C
MANGROVES
N

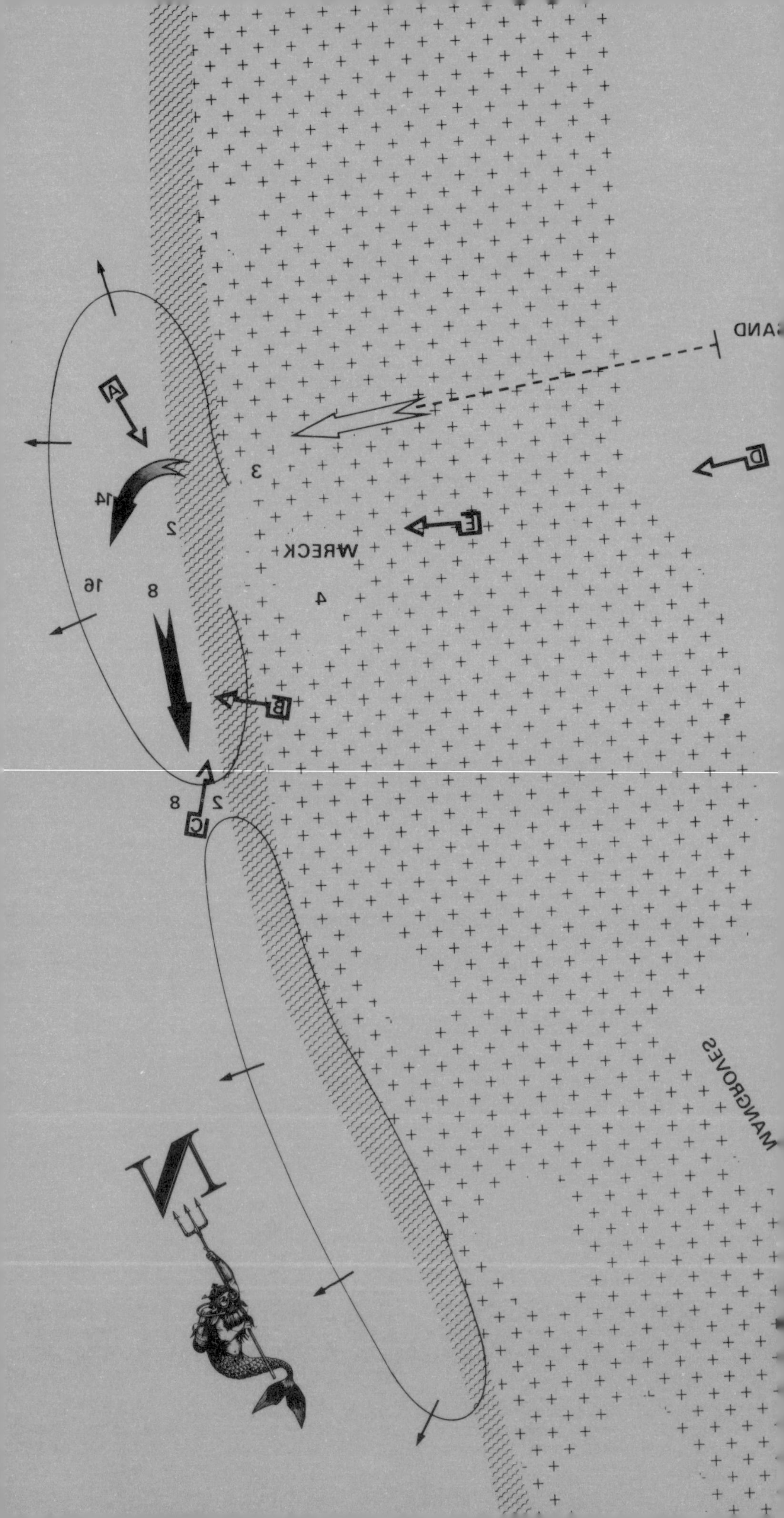

MANGROVES
WRECK
A
B
C
D
E
3
2
14
16
8
4
2
8

SHORA EL MANQATA

Route No. 15

Ref: 09327364
34°26'00"E 28°12'30"N
Departure: Eilat or Ophira
Road Condition & Route:
See NABEK.

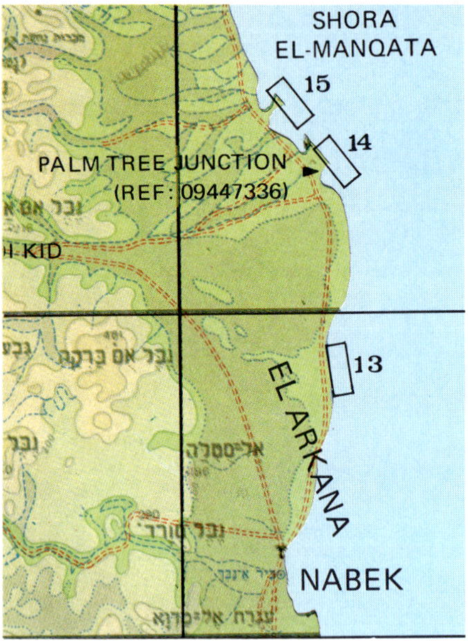

Drive 2 km. (1.3 mi.) north from **The Maria Schröder** and you will see the rich vegetation of many mangroves in the distance (A). This site is the northernmost spot on Earth where they are found growing (B). Immediately before this stand of mangroves, crowding a lagoon, there is a sandy point running eastward to the sea. Turn right and drive onto the point to the shore. Notice how your vehicle is actually parked between two lagoons. Both are very muddy but you can find sand sharks in them and, at high tide, sting rays.

Walking due east into the water off this point you will easily see an underwater canyon. Use it to dive or snorkel through the coral to the seaward edge of the reef table. Then turn south and dive along the reef until you find another canyon of 20 m. (66 ft.) depth leading through the reef into the next lagoon. Explore it to the end and then finish the dive by snorkling north back to your vehicle via that south lagoon.

Special Note: When wading across shallow but muddy lagoon you may encounter a sting ray, waiting for the high tide, by unknowingly stepping on it. Make noise as you cross the lagoon and, if possible, walk with a stick thrown ahead of you.

A →

B →

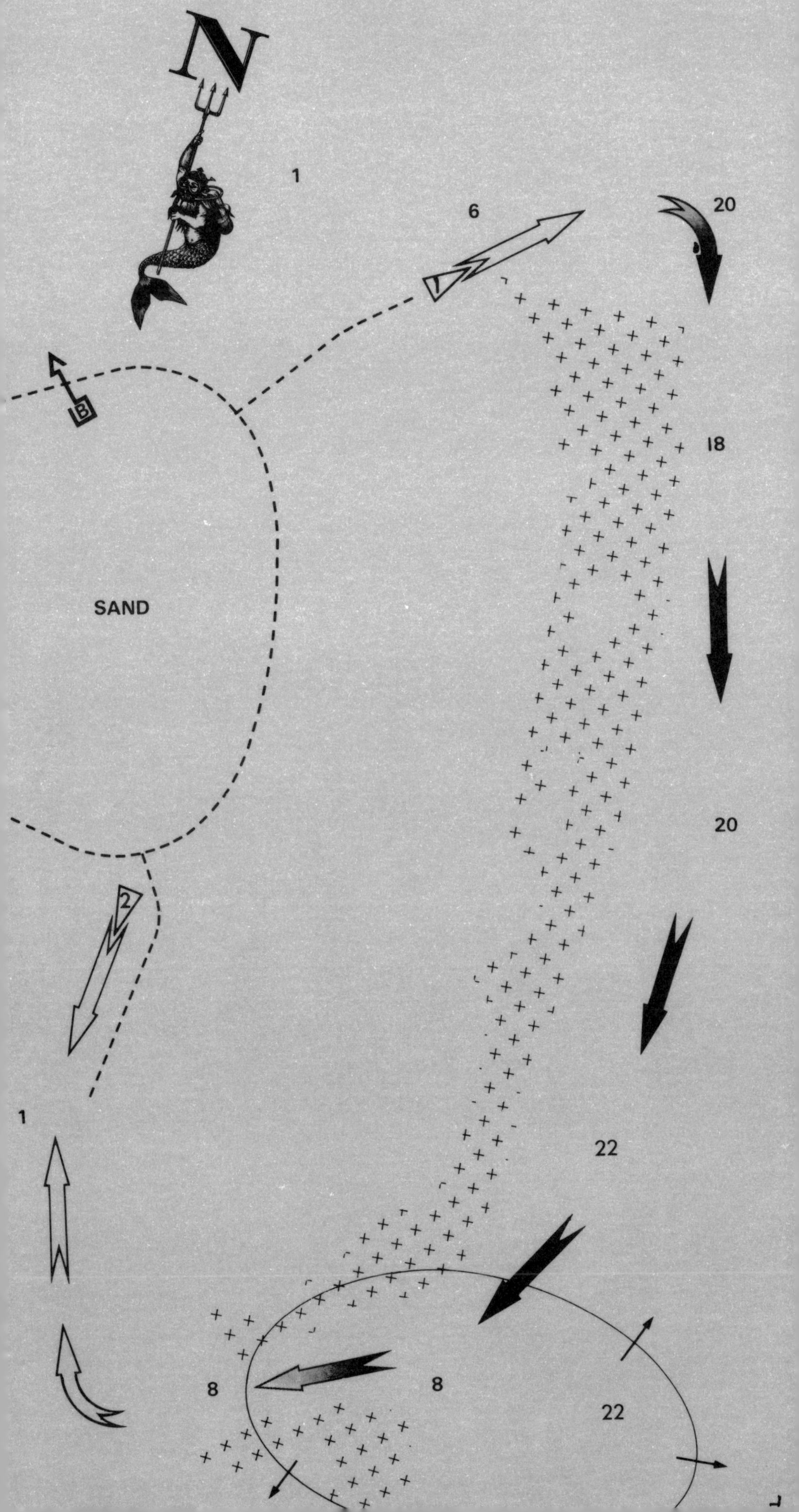
N
1
6
20
B
18
SAND
20
2
1
22
8
8
22

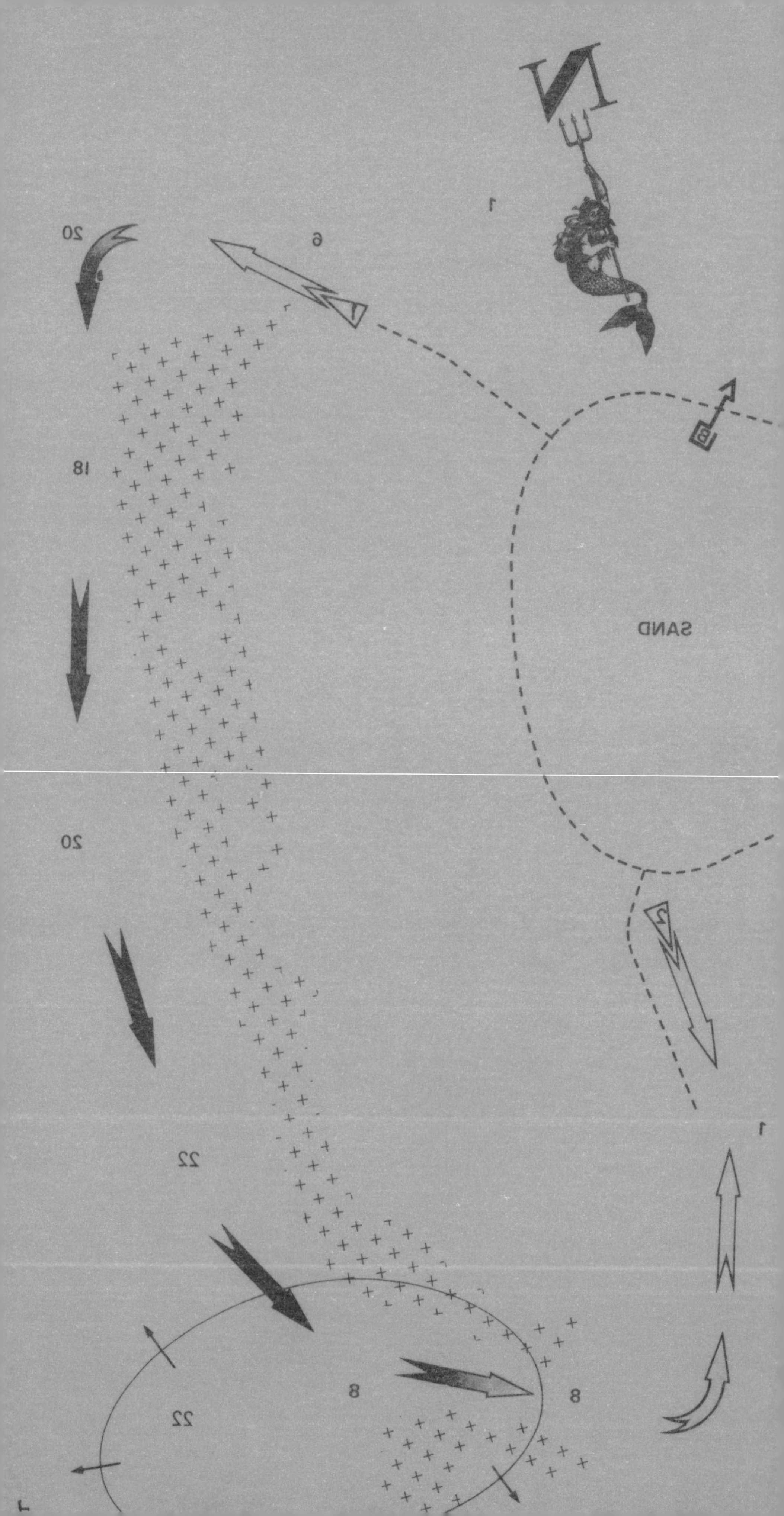
SAND
20
18
20
22
22
8
8
6
1
1

SHARM EL SHEIKH

The Sharm el Sheikh region is by far the richest and most spectacular diving area in the Red Sea.

This expanse of approximately 40 miles of virgin, continuous coral reef is enhanced by dramatic coral drop-offs, aqua-marine bays and coral formations unparalleled in the diving world.

SHARM EL SHEIKH

The coast along the eastern slope of Sinai changes markedly at Ras Nasrani and south as the spacious beaches thin out and vertical cliffs climbing straight up from the sea make their appearance. Beaches get steadily narrower until one finds only bluffs where ancient coral reefs rose up from the ocean floor.

This coastal landscape reaches its dramatic climax on the high bluffs at Ras Muhammed. All of it, in fact, is a solid block of fossil coral lifted from the sea. This great block of antiquarian rock is only connected to the mainland by a long and narrow land bridge about 700–1,000 m. (2,300–3,300 ft.) wide and 3.5 km. (2.2 mi.) long. As the junction for east and west shores of the peninsula, one can stand on Ras Muhammed and note how the high bluffs suddenly disappear. To be replaced again by an alluvial plain, with its salt and mud flats typical of the western shore of Sinai.

Perhaps it was named in honor of the great Moslem prophet Mohammed. (The Arabic word Ras means "head".) It was known to the Romans and they called it "Poseidon" – god of the sea. As the

southernmost point of the Sinai peninsula it divides the Red Sea, like a great fist, and its western shore begins the Gulf of Suez. Follow the eastern shore to the Straits of Tiran and the entrance to the Gulf of Eilat. The elevated table of Ras Muhammed is undulated by rolling hills, the highest being 73 m. (240 ft.) above sea-level. The eastern shore drops vertically to the sea with sheer high cliffs and a narrow, very deep, coral reef running parallel to it. There are no beaches here.

The reef itself encircles the entire head, plunging to 70 m. (230 ft.) depth on the east and 50 m. (165 ft.) on the west. The coral at Ras Muhammed is justifiably world-famous for the variety and vast numbers of marine flora and fauna to be found in, on, and around it. Because of its remarkable conjunction of deep sea and coral habitat, a broad spectrum of coral dwellers and deep-water species are found intermingled in a dynamic and concentrated ecological synthesis. Larger species, from Jack Fish and groupers to rays and sharks, approach the reef easily. Equip yourself both mentally and physically for the reality that you will meet sharks on almost every dive.

The southern tip of Ras Muhammed is actually an island separated from the head by a shallow channel filled with mangroves; remarkable plants living in salt water and breathing through their exposed roots. You will find a wide and long lagoon north of the mangrove channel, much of it intertidal. **Walking** north from the channel to the lagoon you will discover deep crevices in the table containing fresh sea water, evidencing an unknown link with the ocean yet to be investigated.

Caution: the terrain between the mangrove channel and the lagoon can be hazardous for vehicles because of the crevices, and the seemingly firm dry mudflats of the lagoon at low tide will sink under their weight.

How To Get There

Local residents in the area may tell you there are three unpaved routes to Ras Muhammed from Ophira: 1) a road from the Bay of Sharm el-Sheikh along the coast; 2) a road branching from the main highway and passing through Wadi Hashbi; and 3) a road branching from the main Atur highway about 30 km. (19 mi.) west of the Ophira-Atur Junction. The first two

routes, requiring four-wheel drive and an expert driver, are closed to civilian traffic. The third and most comfortable way, always open, will carry standard passenger vehicles: turn left off the Atur asphalt highway (30 km. — 19 mi. — west from Ophira-Atur Junction) onto an unpaved secondary road (Ref: 06186938) running almost straight towards the sea. You will follow this road in the direction of the sea until it turns east (Ref: 06216904). It then continues parallel to the seashore for about 15 km. (9.5 mi.) until reaching rolling hills of white contrasted by a solitary black hill (Ref: 0731685). After passing the black hill you will see a fork in the road: the southern track leads to a stone quay and the mangrove channel while the northern track leads to the shark observatory.

Special Note: Please pay attention to the stones marking the roads on Ras Muhammed and stay within their borders. Attempting a shortcut can easily lead to a day of frustration digging out your vehicle and working it back to the road. Remember, also, Ras Muhammed is totally barren, without water, and not even the Beduin live there. Your journey, therefore, demands meticulous planning with regard to supply and the good condition of your equipment both terrestrial and marine.

DISTANCES

CORAL BEACH — OPHIRA JCT.	214 km. (135 mi.)
OPHIRA JCT. — NA'AMA BAY	7.6 km. (4.8 mi.)
NA'AMA BAY — OPHIRA-ATUR JCT.	5.4 km. (3.4 mi.)
OPHIRA-ATUR JCT. — OPHIRA	2.6 km. (1.6 mi.)
OPHIRA-ATUR JCT. — RAS MUHAMMED JCT. (REF: 016186938)	31 km. (19.5 mi.)
RAS MUHAMMED JCT. — SEA JCT. (REF: 06216904)	3.8 km. (2.4 mi.)
SEA JCT. — BLACK HILL JCT. (REF: 07326850)	15 km. (9.5 mi.)
BLACK HILL JCT. — SHARK OBSERVATORY	3.5 km. (2.2 mi.)
THE QUAY — SHARK REEF	2.5 km. (1.6 mi.)

THE QUAY

Route No. 16
Ref: 07496838
34°14'30"E 27°44'00"N
Departure & Route: Ophira. See "How To Get There".

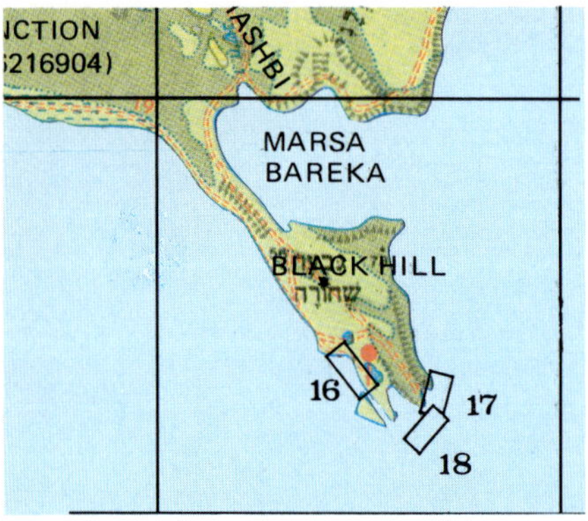

Taking the southern track at the fork after the black hill (Ref: 0731685) the road to the mangrove channel comes very close to the sea and you will recognize the stone quay easily. It crosses a very shallow lagoon and ends on the reef table about 20 m. (66 ft.) from the shore. (The quay was built by Socony-Vacumn Corporation during a search for oil at the beginning of the century.) Standing on the reef table at the seaward edge you will see a vertical reef that ends 40 m. (132 ft.) below. It abounds with coral and fish: huge fan corals, schools of Jack Fish passing by, large groupers, very large Wrasse *(Cheilinus undulatus)*, immense black corals, giant Morray, sea turtles, and the occasional shark or barracuda.

Looking southeast one can see the entrance to the mangrove channel. The beach around the quay is busy with sand crabs during the day. At sunset and throughout the night, however, it is teeming with thousands of hermit crabs having emerged from their hiding places under a thick carpet of mangrove leaves in the lagoon and on the shore.

When diving near the quay you may encounter large white clouds of mineral water mixed with sand that eliminate visibility: a product of hot springs escaping through the reef wall. If you enter one of these clouds turn to open water or continue a few meters to find clear visibility. These springs create sandy banks and caves particularly suitable to the Morray and grouper.

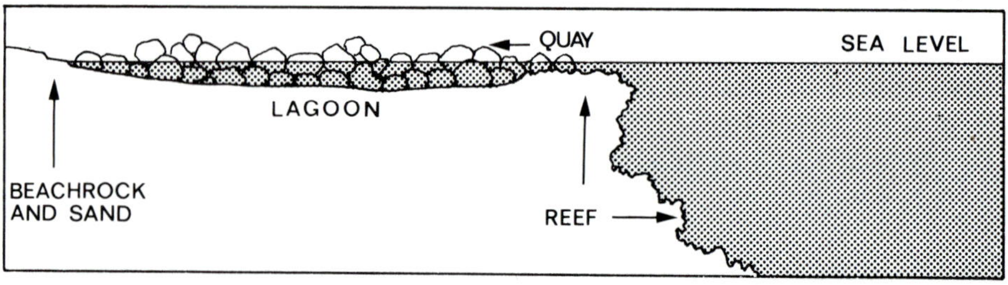

A →

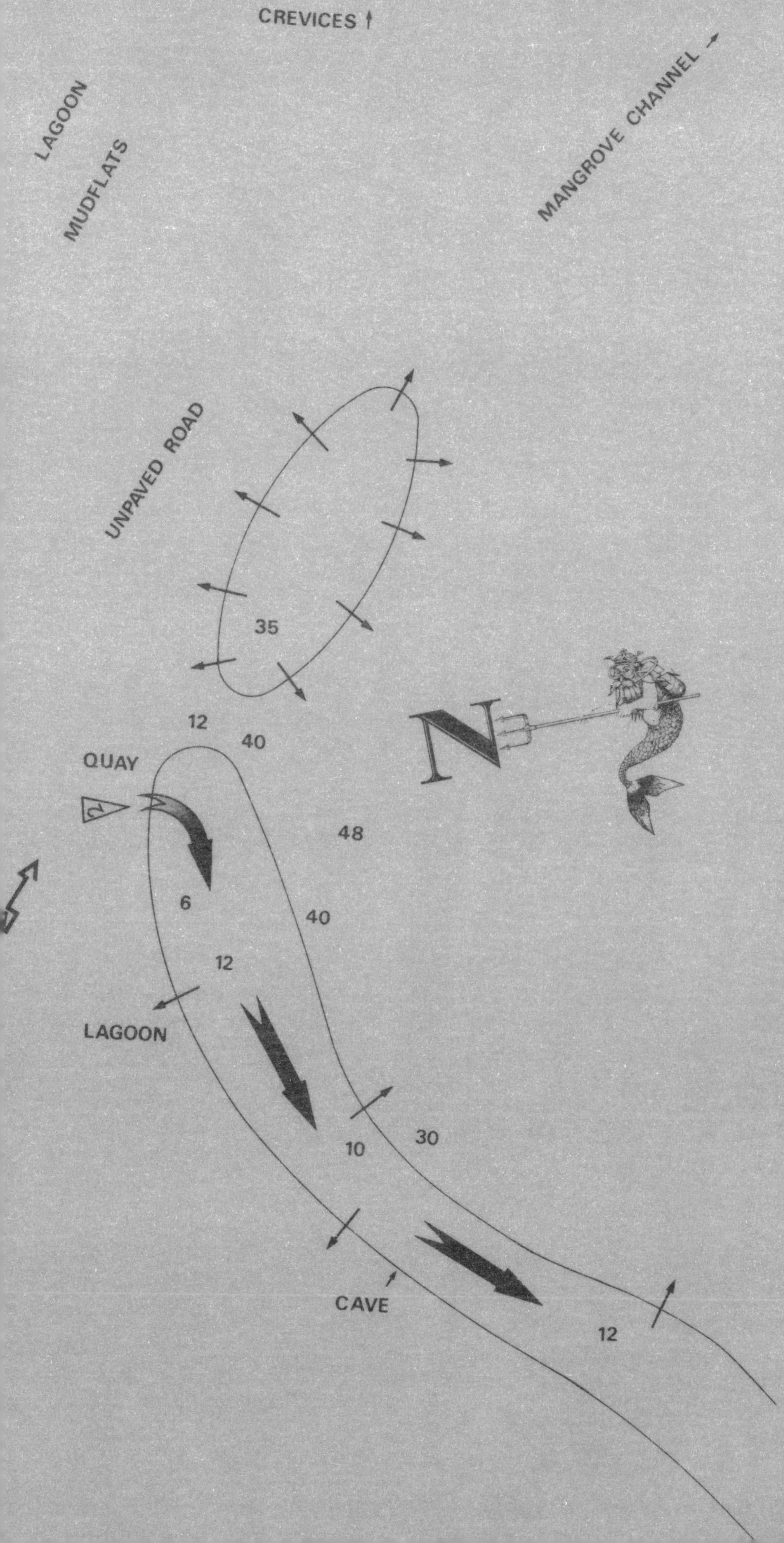
CREVICES
LAGOON
MUDFLATS
MANGROVE CHANNEL
UNPAVED ROAD
35
N
12
40
QUAY
48
6
40
12
LAGOON
10
30
CAVE
12

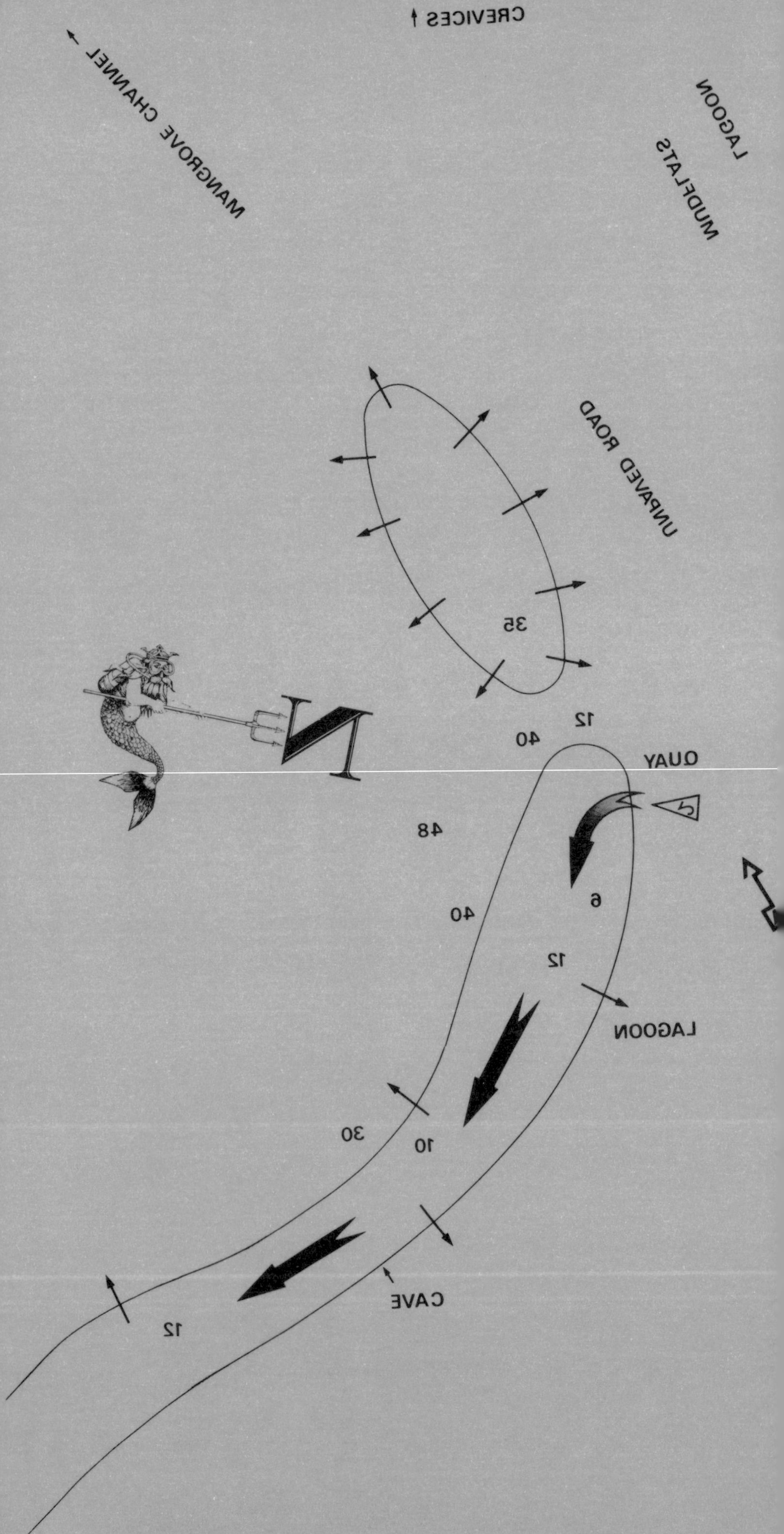
CREVICES
MANGROVE CHANNEL
LAGOON
MUDFLATS
UNPAVED ROAD
35
12
40
QUAY
48
40
6
12
LAGOON
30
10
CAVE
12

SHARK OBSERVATORY

Route No. 17

Ref: 07686830
34°16'00"E 27°44'00"N

Departure & Route:
Ophira.
See "How To Get There".

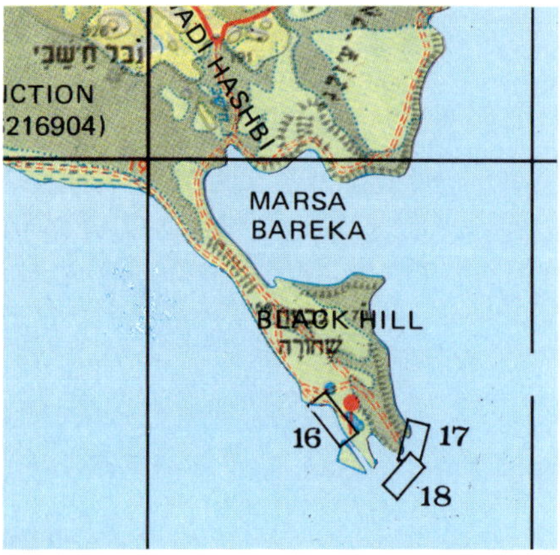

A

B

Taking the northern track at the fork after the black hill (Ref: 0731685) you will arrive at what is unquestionably the most exciting diving site in this volume. (Follow the directions below faithfully for an uneventful arrival.) The reef table is very narrow and its sheer seaward wall vanishes into a deep blue where it stops at 70 m. (231 ft.). It is a vertible treasure trove of coral species guaranteed to drive a marine biologist "up the wall". A word of caution, however, for divers. The fish, the caves, the crevices, and the color tend to so exhilarate . . . they push the explorer deeper and deeper. The fine visibility may also lend a false note of security. Check your air, your depth, your decompression requirements and your distances periodically. This is no ordinary dive.

The shark observatory is a huge rock about 50 m. (165 ft.) high (A). You may climb to the platform on top with the steps beginning in a small cove on its south side. South beyond this cove you will find a square-shaped lagoon. Both north and south sides of this lagoon are filled with rocky ravines (**B**). Take a stroll in the area during the late afternoon, because of the heat, and

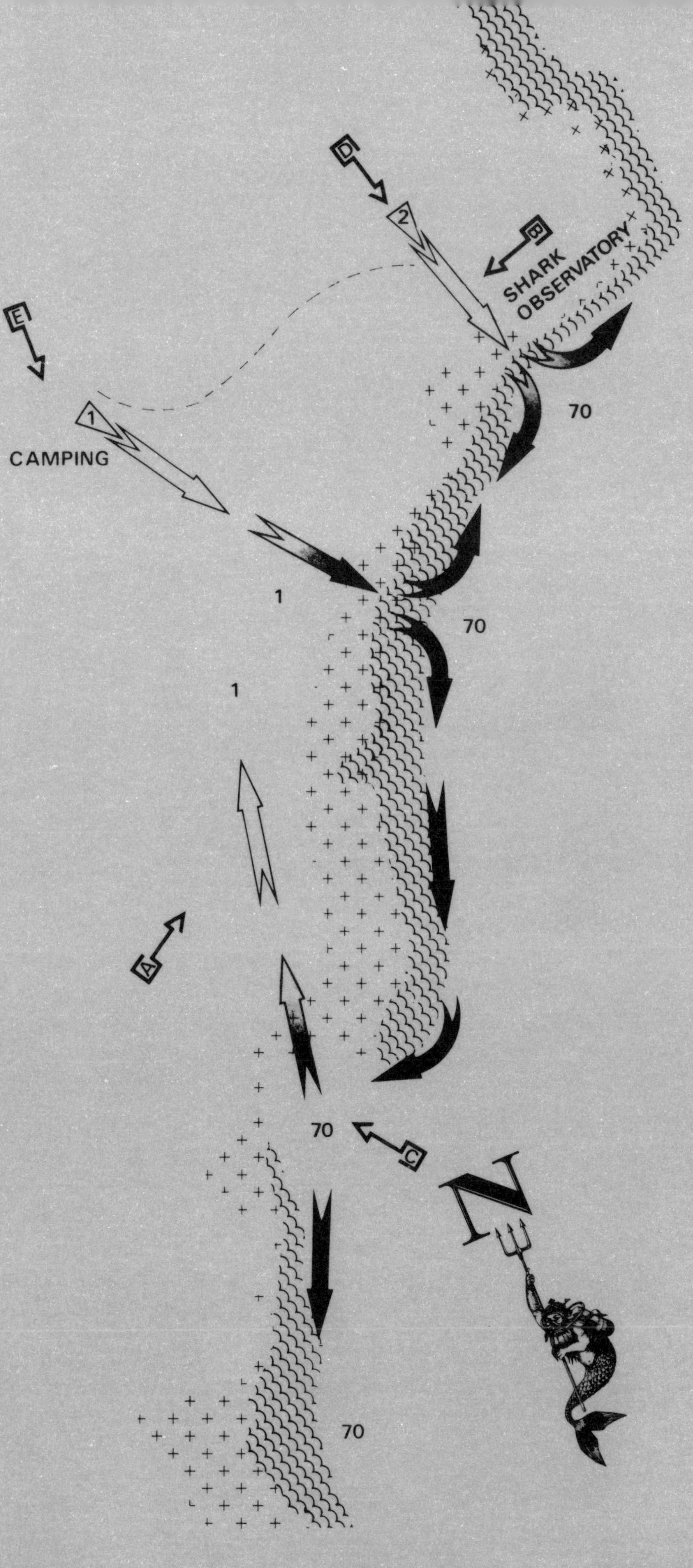
SHARK OBSERVATORY
CAMPING
E
D
2
B
1
70
1
70
1
A
70
C
N
70

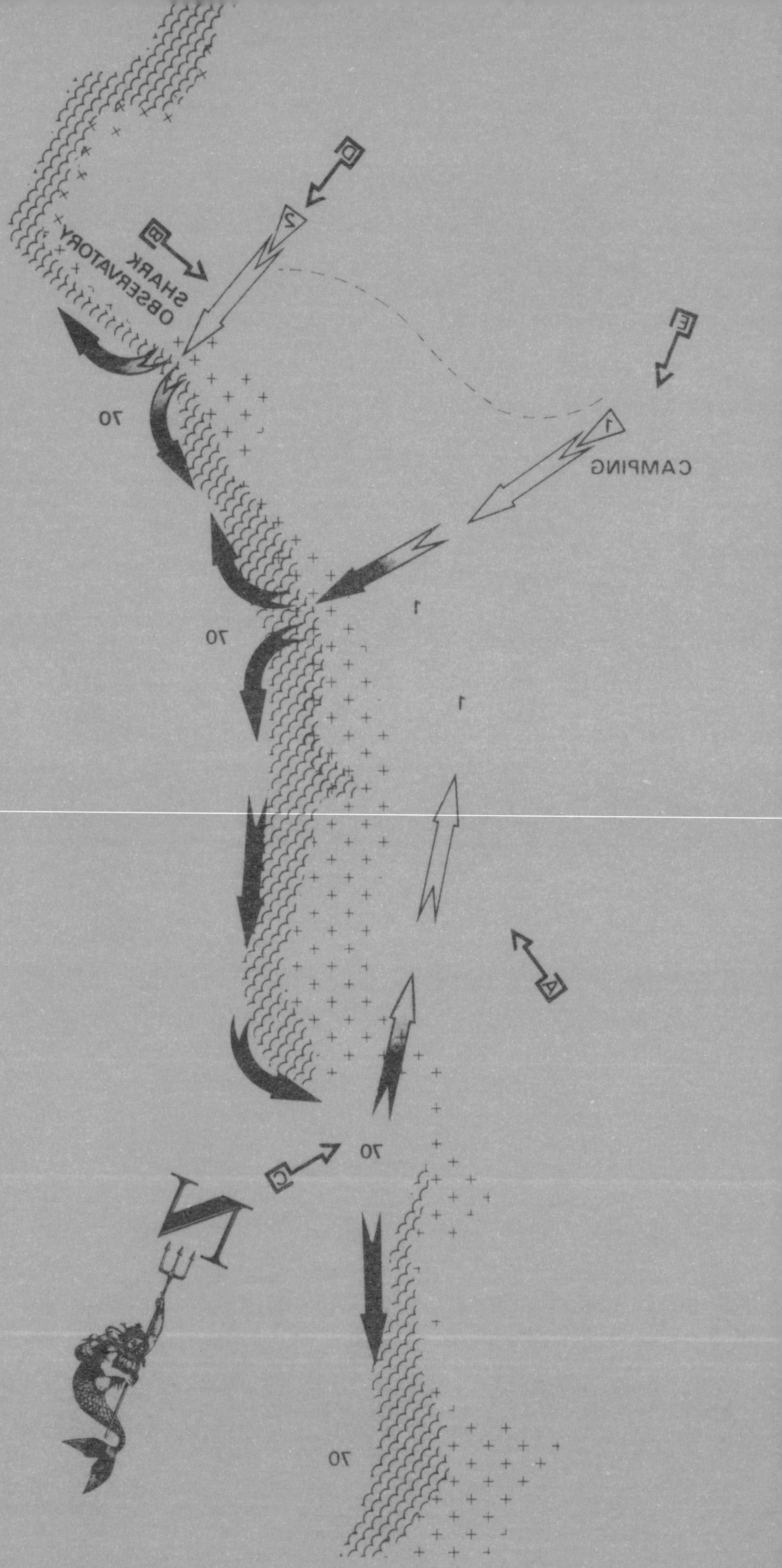
SHARK OBSERVATORY
CAMPING
70
70
70
70
1
1
A
B
C
D
E
1
2

examine the many coral fossils in the ravines around the lagoon before climbing to the observatory for the sunset. Although the steps are difficult, the view is worth the effort. Plus the added, almost magnetic, attraction of easily observing the sharks cruising along the reef. The eastern shore of the lagoon has a beautiful white sandy beach particularly suited for camping. You will find shelters, built of stone and thatched with straw, fireplaces and field toilets. A narrow path leads from the lagoon to the steps of the observatory.

Taking the northern fork after the black hill, you will approach a rough track 3.5 km. (2.2 mi.) further on. Turn onto it and drive carefully. If you want to reach the observatory area do not leave the road or cross over the stones marking it. It leads directly to the campsite at the lagoon. (If, however, you are diving only for the day, turn left just before the lagoon and drive to the small cove on the northern side of the observatory: best entry for a dive is at this north cove with a short distance to the reef table.) When staying for a day or two drive straight to the lagoon and set up camp. Pack your diving gear into a vehicle and drive the few minutes over to the north cove for each dive. You may, of course, snorkel across the lagoon at high tide, not low, but remember to choose the north side with its shorter distance to the reef. It is very difficult to cross the reef table at low tide. When exploring the reef south of the observatory you will find a convenient break leading into the lagoon (C) where you can swim or walk back, depending upon the tide, to the campsite. There is no way to drive or walk on shore to reach the southern end of the lagoon.

When diving north along the reef there is no access to land from the sea. One may rest on the reef table but there is no way up the cliffs to the top of the bluffs. Plan carefully for a return to the cove.

C →

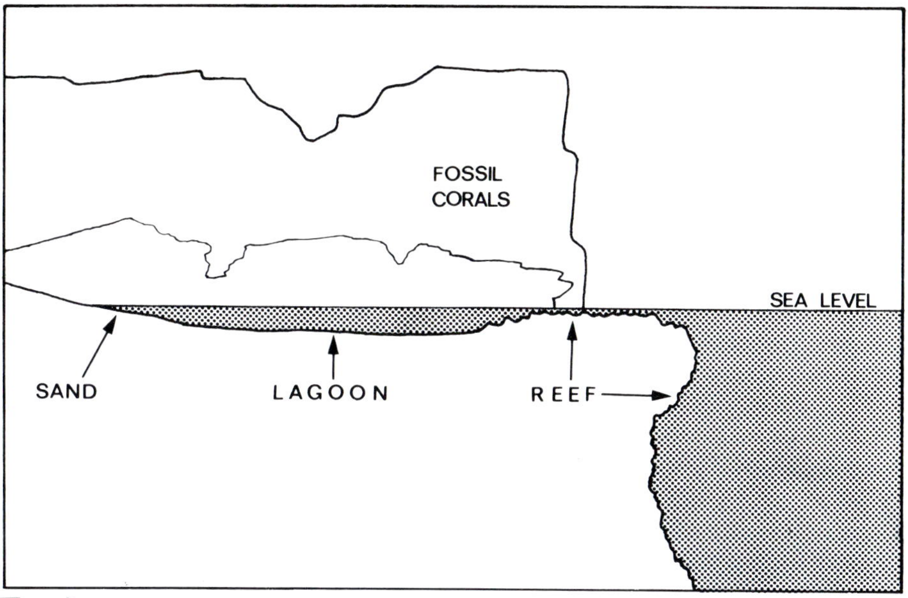

D

E

SHARK REEF

Route No. 18

Departure & Route: Ophira. See "How To Get There".

Continuing on the road past **The Quay** drive to road's end near the southern mouth of the mangrove channel. There are two reef patches in the open sea far off from the reef table and opposite two lagoons. It is possible to swim there but you will meet strong currents in the channel and you must traverse a total distance, over and back, of about 2 km. (1.3 mi.) in shark-infested waters. A "zodiac" or other boat is recommended. It can be easily launched at road's end where there is a convenient cove with a gentle slope permitting you to bring a vehicle to the water's edge. The reefs off this cove are relatively shallow with less marine life than found at other sites on Ras Muhammed. If you want to find sharks, however, this is the place.

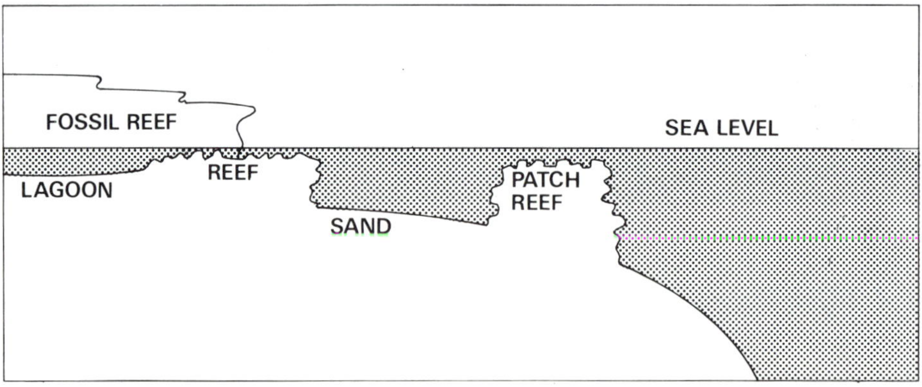

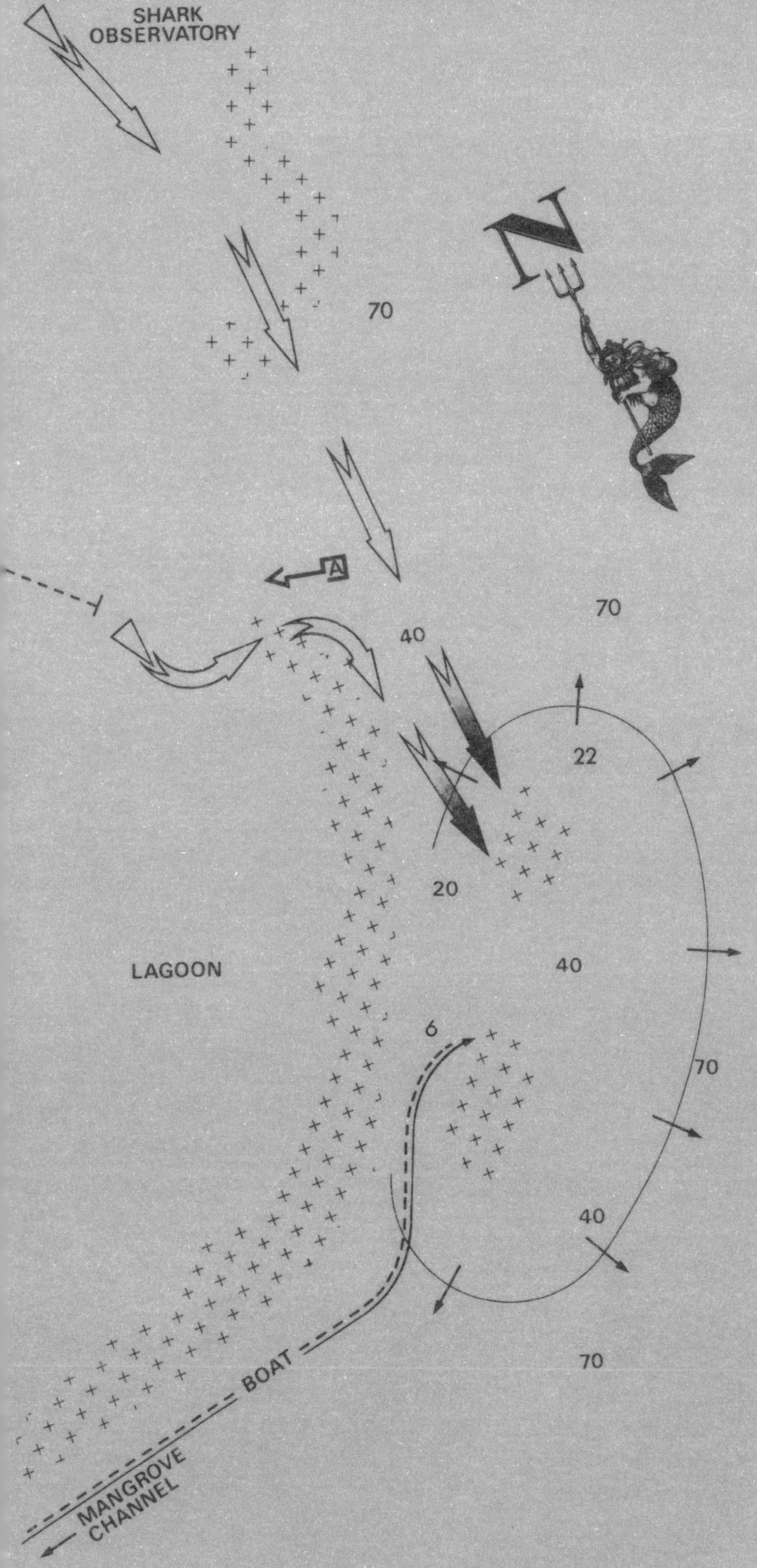
SHARK OBSERVATORY
70
A
70
40
22
20
LAGOON
40
6
70
40
70
BOAT
MANGROVE CHANNEL

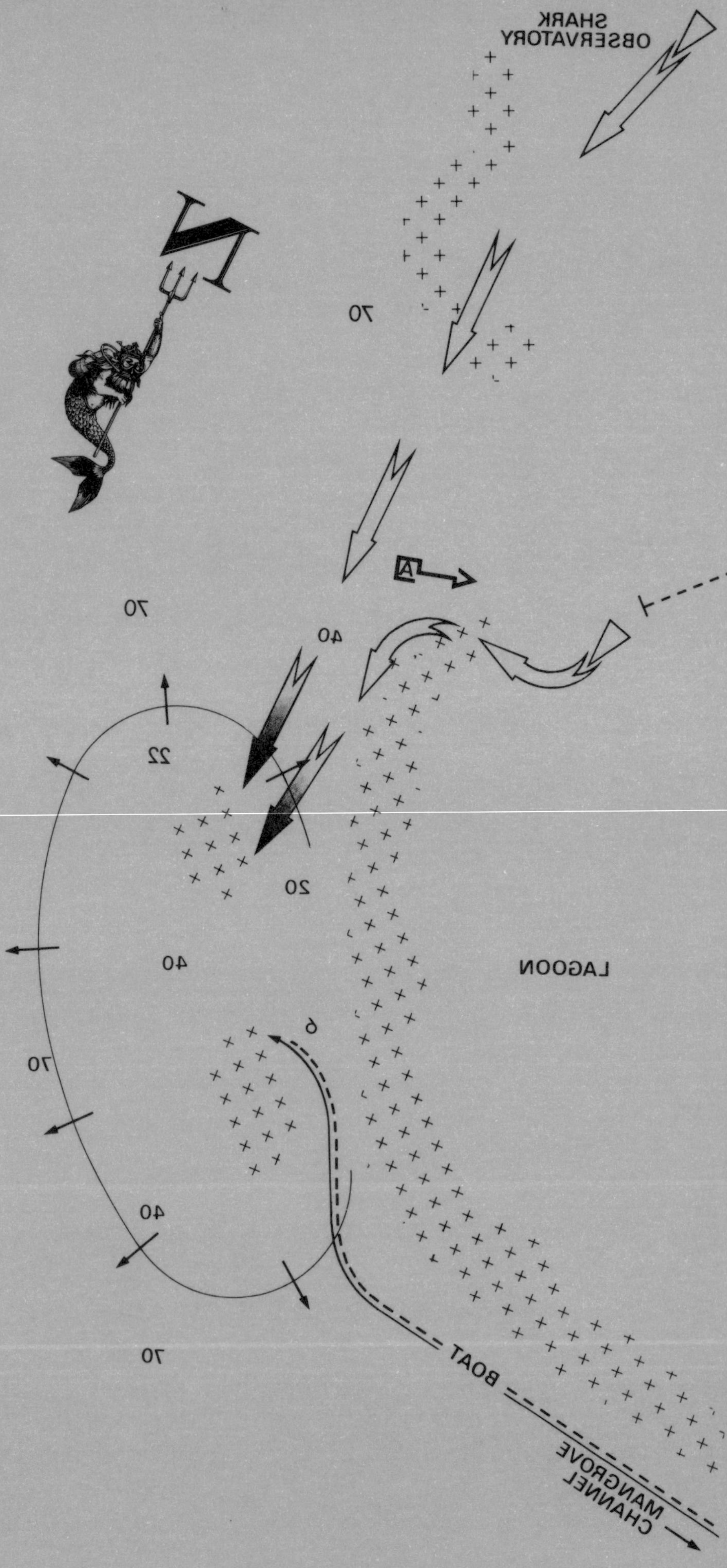
SHARK
OBSERVATORY
70
A
70
40
22
20
40
LAGOON
9
70
40
70
BOAT
MANGROVE
CHANNEL

Coral World
Underwater
Observatory
and
Aquarium
Even if you dive yourself, a visit to the Underwater Observatory is more than just an optional extra! Study a dazzling array of fish at leisure in the comfort of the Underwater Observatory.
UNDERWATER
OBSERVATORY
RESTAURANT
TURTLE AND RAY POOL
MUSEUM & AQUARIUM
GIFT SHOP
SHARK POOL
CORAL REEF TANK
Open daily
from 8:30 a.m.
Tel: (059) 76666.

FISH INDEX

Our oceans are the most densely populated regions on this planet. And yet the least known. They support a range of evolutionary adaptations, both in terms of physiology and in function, representing the most primitive forms of life on earth to some of the most intelligent and complex. Till today the seas contain vast areas, in geological and zoological terms, that remain unknown and still awaiting investigation.

There are about 1,000 identified species of fish in the Gulf of Eilat in addition to an impressive spectrum of invertebrates from corals and crustacea to sponges. This index has been organized to present some 100 of the marine species most commonly found by the diver. The specimens, therefore, are chosen according to this context and not that of a classic zoological discipline. Most of the entries are coral dwellers, living in or near the reef habitat, and can be found in almost every tropical sea around the globe. For convenience in identification they are divided into three general groups: 1) territorial — remaining at one specific place; 2) semi-territorial — staying within a specific feeding zone; and 3) nomadic — feeding along the reef, most of them in open water.

Coral fish are famous for brilliant colors and well developed camouflage while their anatomy has adapted for greater ease in feeding in and around the reefs. Open water species are, of course, larger and have evolved a hydrodynamic shape providing for powerful and rapid movement.

There is one important and most basic rule to observe whenever diving in tropical waters: do not touch or play with any species that remains passive and does not attempt to flee when you reach out to touch it. Any mobile marine animal possessing this characteristic has some kind of natural defense be it poison, mild or deadly, unusual color or form, or an unpleasant taste. Unless you are a specialist with the necessary zoological background — don't guess. In any case, the recommended weapon in a diver's hand is . . . a camera.

CORAL FISH

Dascyllus aruanus

This tiny Coral Fish adds much to the shimmering beauty of the diver's landscape. Their small size, 4 cm. (2 in.), is their natural defense against predators. They congregate in schools of 5 to 20 and prefer to reside in the tortuous and many-branched corals like *Acropora, Pocillopora, Stylophora* and *Seriatopora.* Both these corals and their attendant fish are usually discovered in lagoons or on shallow bottom near the reef. They never venture more than a meter or two (3–7 ft.) from their coral patch and vanish rapidly inside when endangered. They feed on plankton ciab arriving with the current.

THREE-SPOTTED CORAL FISH

Dascyllus trimaculatus

A little different from the usual Coral Fish, this particular species use the anemone as shelter when young and can be recognized by the three white spots they later lose in adulthood. When full-grown they leave the anemone and then prefer to live between rocks and large corals. They grow to 7–8 cm. (3–3.5 in.).

BLUE GREEN CHROMIS

Chromis caeruleus

These greenish-blue Coral Fish live in schools of a few hundred and generally prefer *Acropora* as their habitat. About 3 cm. (1.5 in.) in adulthood.

BROWN-WHITE REEF FISH

Chromis dimidiatus

Although a tiny reef resident, 7–8 cm. (3–3.5 in.), it can easily be recognized by a distinctive two-color pattern: the first-half is brown and the second-half white. Always discovered near the reef in schools.

FRIDMANI FISH

Pseudochromis fridmani

This tiny 5 cm. (2 in.) fish is easily recognized by its prominent pale violet color. More populous to the south in the Gulf, they live in tiny crevices on the seaward walls of the reef. (Discovered by David Frid-man.)

CLOWN FISH

Amphiprion bicinctus

The habitat and habits of Clown Fish demonstrate a perfect symbiotic relationship with sea anemones where the fish provide the food and the anemones guarantee the security. Usually seen in pairs and always near a particular anemone, only they are immune to its poisonous tentacles. This fish brings food to its particular host and will fiercly attack any intruder, regardless of size, to protect its security zone. Approaching within a meter (3.3 ft.) or less of their "home", divers are often startled and then amused by this relatively small species fearlessly attacking their diving mask. The younger fish prefer *Radianthus sp.* as their symbiotic partner while adults prefer *Girostoma sp.* Females lay their eggs on rock or reef covered with these Coelenterata. At night the Clown Fish can usually be found hiding in their tentacles.

SHARP-NOSED PUFFER

Canthigaster coronatus

Paradoxically enough, this member of the Puffer family is best recognized by its bulging and shiny eyes. These small 7 cm. (3 in.) fish are usually seen in the reef area and live in pairs.

DAMSEL FISH

Five vertical black stripes, often with a pale yellow background, give the Sergeant Major its name. You find them feeding along the reef in large schools with the average mature adult measuring about 12 cm. (5 in.). Their schools on "Moses Rock" at Coral Beach near Eilat are fearless and will join your dive. The Gray Damsel is usually found with the Sergeant Major.

Sergeant Major *Abudefduf saxatilis*

Grey Damsel Fish
Abudefduf leucogaster

EMPEROR FISH
ANGEL FISH

These territorial dwellers are considered the most strikingly beautiful and magnificent specimens to be found in tropical waters, always to be seen within close range of their cave-abode. The Emperor manifests a dramatic change in both color and pattern from youth to adulthood.

Peacock Angel fish *Pygoplites diacanthus*

Emperor Fish (adult) *Pomacanthus imperator*

Emperor Fish (young) *Pomocanthus imperator*

Queen Angel Fish *Pomacanthodes maculosus*

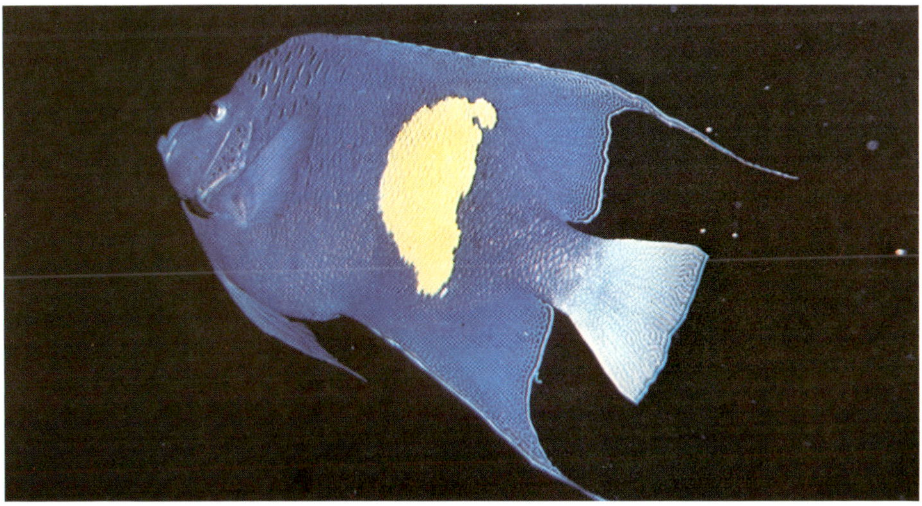

BUTTERFLY FISH

This very colorful, well-known and unusually aesthetic family is a typical reef resident, seen by their thin bodies that provide manueverability for feeding in the narrow breaks and crevices of the coral. Usually seen in pairs or small schools, these nomads find food and feed within a limited range and then move on – a familiar sight throughout the length of the Gulf.

Common Butterfly fish *Chaetodon chrysurus*

Striped Butterfly fish *Chaetodon fasciatus*

Blacktail Butterfly fish *Chaetodon austriacus*

Lemon Butterfly fish *Chaetodon semilarvatus*

ANGEL ANTENNA FISH

Heniochus intermedius

Angel Antenna fish are easily identified by the extended dorsal fin that gave them their name and are cousins of the Butterfly Fish. *H. acuminiatus* congregate in large schools in open water and may be seen at considerable depth. *H. intermedius*, however, prefer the inter-coral habitat within the reef where they are found swimming in pairs.

GOLD FISH

Anthias sp.

A very common tiny fish living in huge schools of hundreds and thousands usually found on coral patches. South along the Gulf, however, they are also found in the cliffs of the deep-water reef. Males are reddish-purple and the females only red.

BOX FISH

Ostracion cubicus

Evolution has given these unusually photogenic fish an unexpected geometrical body supported by tough, bony and armored-like skin that exudes a poison for protection against predators. These solitary feeders, not gregarious fish, can be found both along and inside the reef and, occasionally, in open water. The Box Fish is, of course, rectangular in form while the Trunk Fish is triangular. These shy but slow swimmers are, once found, easy to catch in the camera lens.

SURGEON FISH (DOCTOR FISH)

This generic name actually applies to and is commonly used for several species found along the entire Gulf reef. The name derives from the two unique spines found at the base of the tail, as sharp as a surgeon's scalpel, they can project for defense. *Z. xanthurus* is easily identified by a deep purple-blue torso and orange tail. *A. sohal* exhibits blue stripes covering the entire body contrasted by its clearly visible yellow "scalpels". Surgeon Fish reach about 50 cm. (1.6 ft.) length in adulthood. *A. sohal* are generally found in the wave action at the deep-water edge of the reef table.

Purple Surgeon Fish *Zebrasoma xanthurus*

Sail-finned Surgeon Fish *Zebrasoma veliferum*

Surgeon Fish *Acanthurus sohal*

Naso is the largest of this group and can easily reach 60 cm. (2 ft.). *N. litoratus* is quickly distinguished by its strong colors: the body is purple, brown and green while its forehead, fins and tail are orange.

N. unicornis is famous for the long horn emerging from its head. Both can be found in the southern part of the Gulf where they prefer to feed near deep-water reef.

Striped Face Unicornfish *Naso litoratus*

Unicornfish *Naso unicornis*

TRIGGER FISH

These remarkable fish are found along all the reefs and particularly near reef patches. They were commonly named for the trigger-spine that pops up from their back when they are threatened, much like a barb on a hook, making it difficult if not impossible to pull them from a wedged position in the coral. The midnight-blue *Odonus niger,* largest of the Trigger Fish and reaching about 60 cm. (2 ft.), has three distinctive behavioral characteristics. You may come upon one of them digging on sandy bottom in almost vertical position much like standing on its head. *Odonus* may become aggressive when a diver appears, extend its trigger and approach the explorer in a pseudo-menacing fashion. They can also be found at night, interestingly enough, sleeping on their sides.

Trigger Fish *Pseudobalistes fuscus*

Picasso Fish *Rehinecanthus asasi*

Hemibalistes chrysoptera

Striped Trigger Fish *Balistapus undulatus*

WRASSE

One of the largest and most common families found along the Gulf with active and energetic personalities, moving without stop during the entire day. *C. undulatus* may grow to a magnificent 120 cm. (4 ft.) and weigh as much as 150 kilos (330 lbs.). Search for them in open water at Ras Muhammed.

The Rainbow Fish is the most familiar Wrasse from Eilat to the southern tip of Sinai and one of those species distinguished by sharp color changes during their life span (see photographs). This unusually gregarious coral feeder may reach 60 cm. (2 ft.) and if fed by a diver may often follow him for the remainder of the dive.

Common Rainbow Fish *Thalassoma ruppelli*

Napoleon Fish *Cheilinus undulatus*

Rainbow Fish (young) *Coris angulata*

Rainbow Fish (intermediate) *Coris angulata*

Rainbow Fish (adult) *Coris angulata*

Cheilinus lundularis

Brown-white Wrasse *Bodianus anthioides*

PARROT FISH *Scarus sp.*

A truly general common name covering an incredible variety of families and species seen along the entire reef. A prominent fish because of its remarkable montage of distinctive "kitsch" colors, particularly the males. They can grow to 60 cm. (2 ft.) and are easily identified by the jaw and teeth, similar to that of a parrot, used to break the corals. Divers hear the crushing noise clearly as they eat their daily quota of polyps. Caution: although not aggressive they can easily bite off the tip of a finger if provoked by a careless diver.

BIRD FISH *Gomphosus coeruleus*

A strange and beautiful creature named for its elongated mouth similar to the beak of a bird. Growing to about 25 cm. (10 in.), the male is colored green and the female brownish-yellow. Picture: a female specimen photographed with a Goat Fish.

RABBIT FISH *Siganus sp.*

A common family found along the Gulf with a few species living in large schools. *Siganus stellatus*, however, only travel in pairs. Known as a very tasty fish. Beware of the spine on the forepart of its dorsal fin: not a dangerous poison but painful.

LION FISH

A most famous fish because of its remarkable anatomy and brilliant colors. They are known by several other common names: fire fish, sun fish, zebra fish, turkey fish, etc. All exhibit vertical stripes of red, pink, white, brown, or black. A distinguishing feature of the Lion Fish is their very large fan-like pectoral fins. They are both incredibly attractive and potentially dangerous not only to the smaller fish they prey upon but to divers as well, although for different reasons. These passive, almost drifting, swimmers suddenly dart forth with amazing speed to devour a small fish innocently swimming by. The innocent diver finning by may be tempted to touch one of them but please remember: Permanent poison spines on their dorsal fins automatically eject upon touch. Shock and extreme pain follows. This explains why the Lion Fish is totally uninterested in, indifferent to, and unafraid of divers. Observe, enjoy and photograph but keep a respectful and reasonable distance. The pectoral fins of *Pterois radiata* are very long but do not give the impression of a fan, being individual and unlinked as its scientific name suggests.

Special Note: Most fish that are not afraid of a larger species (including you) have developed some kind of natural protection apart from flight or aggressive behavior – unusual color or patterns; an unappetizing flavor; or some kind of poison be it mild or strong.

Common Lion Fish *Pterois volitans*

Fire Lion Fish *Pterois radiata*

SCORPION FISH
STONE FISH

Contrary to popular mythology about sharks, the Scorpion Fish and Stone Fish are the two most dangerous reef residents for divers. Stingers on their upper dorsal fins, containing a strong poison, spring forth automatically under pressure. The unwary diver must touch or step upon them to activate their possibly fatal defensive action. These passive predators, like the Lion Fish, neither attack not approach the explorer. Their great danger derives from behavioral and physiological adaptations. They lie motionless on the bottom, on the reef, or rock, waiting for an unsuspecting fish to swim past while maintaining a perfect camouflage with their environment. They do, indeed, look like stones!

Special Note: Unless you have done your zoological and botanical homework thoroughly, a basic rule to follow in tropical waters is to avoid touching the flora and fauna of the reef and remember to wear good tennis shoes or fins, obviously without holes.

Scorpion Fish *Scorpaena sp.*

Stone Fish *Synanceia verrucosa*

GROUPER

The Grouper is another predator famous among salt-water chefs for its fine flavor. It is one of the most important and largest of families found among the reef population. This common name encompasses a wide variety of species, many growing to huge size, found along the Gulf at many different depths and even in the reef caves. Explore for the larger species in the southern part of the Gulf and you may find one more than a meter (3.3 ft.) long.

Epinephelus fasciatus

Cephalopolis argus

Variola louti

Epinephelus sp.

GOAT FISH

One of the most common and numerous types to be encountered throughout the diver's entire exploratory range. The title includes several species, most of them living in schools. They prefer sandy bottom near the reef where they can dig for food. Eatable.

Pseudupineus macronema

Upeneus molucensis Young & Adult

SOLDIER FISH

Hiding in the darkness of cave, crevice and grotto during the day, these nocturnal predators begin the hunt at twilight. Quickly recognized by their red tones and large eyes characteristic of nocturnal feeders.

Soldier Fish *Holocentrus spinifer*

Crowned Soldier Fish *Holocentrus diadema*

BIG EYE

Priacanthus arenatus

Usually found drifting motionlessly near their lair, these nocturnal predators are found only in the reef area. They change rapidly from red to silver, as seen in this picture, when exposed to light.

TRUMPET FISH

Fistularia petimba

As a relative of the Pipe Fish this peculiar animal also has a long pipe-shaped body ending, however, with a trumpet-like head. These hunters specialize in smaller fish and live near the reef where they change their color to match the surroundings. Two pictures: one daylight and the other nocturnal.

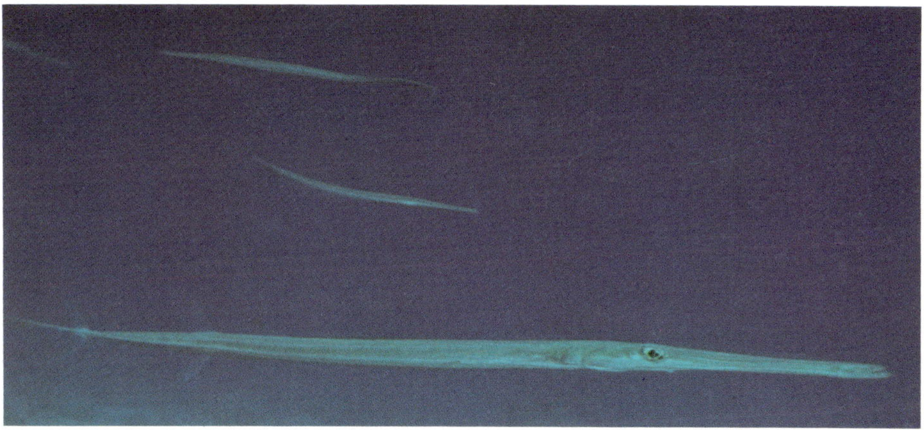

NEEDLE FISH

Belone sp.

Look just a few centimeters below the surface to find them; where they spend the greater part of their lives in small schools chasing larger schools of even smaller fish. They were named for their long thin bodies with a mouth tapering like a needle. Eatable.

BARRACUDA

Sphyraena sp.

The Barracuda maintains an undeserved dangerous reputation around the world. In the Gulf, for example, there is no attack on record in the last 25 years. The young live in huge schools but separate at maturity and become solitary hunters. The more successful of their breed can survive to reach 100–150 cm. (3.3–5.0 ft.). Eatable. Famous for remarkable bursts of speed, you may discover one following you with great curiosity just below the ocean surface. Picture: Barracuda at a "cleaning station" (see Cleaner Fish).

CLEANER FISH (BARBER FISH) *Labroides dimidiatus*

One of the most fascinating and rewarding sites on the diver's underwater itinerary is the "cleaning station". The owners and proprietors of the "station" (some divers refer to the location as "the barber shop") are the Cleaner Fish, usually in pairs, that reach about 10 cm. (8 in.) at maturity. *L. dimidiatus* play an essential role in the reef ecology by eating most parasites attaching themselves to the skin, teeth and gills of fish. All fish recognize the role of the Cleaner and the most dangerous of predators come to their "shop" for "a shave". Each species has its own particular signal for indicating a request for service. Two examples: the Grouper arrives and opens both its mouth and gills while the Goat Fish stands either on its head or tail. One may even observe a Cleaner Fish disappearing into the mouth of a large predator and then exit when its job is done. Each Cleaner Fish stays within its own particular cleaning district on the reef. Although not a Cleaner Fish, *Aspidontus sp.* is an almost perfect replica that even imitates the Cleaner's movements as a ploy to get near a potential victim. When successful, *Aspidontus* suddenly takes a bite of the victim's eye, or other soft spot, and then dashes away.

JACK FISH *Caranx sp.*

These solitary feeders can occasionally be seen in schools. Larger examples of this silver-colored fish are found in the south.

FROG FISH *Antennarius sp.*

The Frog Fish is a master of camouflage and the unwary diver may easily pass them by. This remarkable predator matches perfectly with its environment except for its extended antenna ending with a bouncing ball on the end. *Antennarius* utilize their remarkable biological adaptation to attract the attention of small fish and then bring them near, before snatching them in one bite.

LIZARD FISH *Synodus sp.*

Wherever you dive in the Gulf you may find the Lizard Fish lying motionless on the bottom, coral, or a rock. Settle down quietly and wait. When a smaller fish comes past watch them leap suddenly from their platform and devour it.

CROCODILE FISH *Platycephalus sp.*

On sandy bottom near the reef or under a coral outcrop one may discover what many consider the most interesting species visually and, therefore, photographically: the reptilian-like Crocodile Fish. They also lie motionless and snatch their prey as they swim near. The Crocodile may reach 1 m. (3.3 ft.) in length. Not to be confused with the Scorpion or Stone fishes.

MORRAY EEL

"Morray eel" is a term applied to several species found in the reefs from Eilat to Ras Muhammed, living in caves and crevices. During the day one seldom sees more than its head or some part of its body. The Morray is a nocturnal predator but, contrary to popular legend, is not poisonous. Nevertheless, they exhibit an aggressive personality combined with strong sharp teeth and a painful bite worthy of your respect and distance. Caution: Don't play with them. *G. nudvomer* the largest and more commonly seen in the south, can reach a total length of 2 m. (6.6 ft.) with a 25 cm. (10 in.) head.

Gymnotorax nudivomer

Sidera grisea

GARDEN EEL

Gorgasia sillneri

Although each eel digs its own individual tunnel-abode, they are found in communities numbering from about a hundred to thousands. There are a few sites along the Gulf where you may find a Garden Eel community. (The best known is near Aqua Sport Diving Centre at Coral Beach.) They prefer sandy bottom at depths from 3–20 m. (10–65 ft.). Thin and long (1 cm. diameter and 60 cm. length), they may be seen during the day if you approach quietly and without agitation. You will discover them waving softly in the current with their heads pointed upstream to collect plankton. When disturbed they sink silently backward into their tunnels with the head disappearing last.

CARDINAL FISH

Apogon Sp.

Cardinals represent a large family of tiny coral fish living in large schools in dim half-lit habitats or at entrances to caves and grottoes. They are active primarily at night.

PUFFER FISH (BLOW FISH)

"Puffer" is another general title that includes many species. This group is one of the most interesting due to a unique capacity for inflating their bodies by swallowing water, much like inflating a balloon, and thereby frightening potential predators. All of the species utilize this remarkable adaptation for survival, some with spines and others with poison excreted from their skin. Puffer Fish grow to a maximum length of about 60 cm. (2 ft.) and are solitary feeders along the reef or in deeper water. Be careful: their mouth is one large incisor and can easily bite off a finger.

Black-spotted Puffer
Arothron stellatus

Globe Fish
Arothron diadematus

Spiny Globe Fish *Cyclichthys echinatus*

White spotted Puffer Fish *Arothron hispidus*

RASED FISH

Pempheris oualensis

The Rased Fish live in large schools in the deep caves of the reef, emerging only at night to search for food in open water. At maturity they may reach 20 cm. (8 in.).

BLUE FISH

Caesio lunaris

Seen along the entire Gulf in open water near the reefs, Blue Fish move in large schools that never enter the corals. Although predominately an incandescent blue, the end of their tail is speckled in dark blue and white. Eatable.

SEAHORSE
PIPE FISH

The Sea Horse family is interesting, amusing and strange. Males, for example, carry the fertilized eggs in a pouch and give delivery of their young. These vertical swimmers live on sandy bottoms supporting a plentitude of plant life and, therefore, prefer quiet coves or bays where they can usually be found sitting with their tails wrapped around a convenient branch. A relative of theirs, the Pipe Fish, prefer sandy bottom near the reef.

Seahorse *Hippocampus histrix* →

Pipe Fish *Synganthus sp.* ↓

ELECTRIC RAY

This ray is completely round with a diameter that can reach 30 cm. (1 ft.). They may generate sufficient electric power to register 100 volts. Usually found on sandy bottom, completely covered, they utilize their voltage to stun small fish. Not extremely dangerous to divers but they can give a strong shock.

Torpedo marmorata

REEF STING RAY

The most common ray in the reef ecology. They are dangerous for divers because they lie on sandy bottom and can be stepped upon. The poisonous stinger in the first-third of its tail may cause extreme but not fatal pain. They lash out with their tail when disturbed much in the same manner as a desert scorpion.

Taenuria lymma

EAGLE RAY

Myliobatis aquila

This aesthetic swimmer, much like a graceful bird, does not bury itself in the sand and is generally found in open water. They have been known, however, to enter the reef lagoons during high tide.

The Eagle Ray is dangerous because of its powerful poison but it is not deadly. If you spot this ray then be careful and keep searching for its partner; they are usually found in pairs.

Spotted Eagle Ray *Aetobatus narinari*

Easily distinguished from other rays by the white rings on its back. This graceful elegant flyer prefers open water and is seldom seen in the reef area.

GUITAR SHARK

Rhinobatus sp.

A cartilaginuous fish belonging to the order RAJAE, standing midway between sharks and rays. Looking but not flying like a ray, it swims as a fish with trail strokes.

MANTA RAY

Largest in the family of rays, the Manta can easily reach a wing spread of 6 m. (20 ft.) and weigh up to 2 tons. Despite this enormous creature's gentle movements and the graceful appearance of a slow flying bird it has the capability of leaping several meters (yards) into the air. They are not dangerous because unlike other rays they do not possess a poisonous stinger in the tail.

Manta sp.

Sharks of the Red Sea

1. BLACKTIP REEF SHARK *(Carcharhinus melanopterus)*
2. GREAT HAMMERHEAD *(Sphyrna mokarran)*
3. SANDBAR SHARK *(Carcharhinus plumbeus)*
4. SHORTFIN MAKO *(Isurus oxyrinchus)*
5. MOSES SHARK *(Mustelus mosis)*

6. WHITETIP REEF SHARK	*(Triaenodon obesus)*
7. TIGER SHARK	*(Galeocerdo cuvier)*
8. LEOPARD SHARK	*(Stegostoma fasciatum)*
9. WHALE SHARK	*(Rhiniodon typus)*
10. THRESHER SHARK	*(Alopias vulpinus)*

SHARKS

Like all tropical oceans the Red Sea supports a wide variety of sharks including some of the most dangerous. Nevertheless, there is no shark attack against a diver on record for the Gulf. In fact, only one major attack of any kind has occured in the last 25 years and that to a swimmer in open, relatively deep water several hundred meters from the shore.

The authors, however, do not want visiting divers to break this remarkable record. Therefore, treat the shark with the honor and respect it deserves.

The basic rules for protection are very simple. First of all, stay cool and don't panic – in most cases a single shark will run away from you. In his eyes you are a rather large fish. But solitary sharks frequently return with several colleagues, so continue your dive and remain alert after the loner disappears. A school of sharks are dangeous, particularly when they exhibit behavior indicating nervousness and/or excitement. The best response is to leave the water finning slowly and smoothly without agitation. **Do not ascend to the surface.** Avoid spasmodic, sudden or exaggerated movements. If in open water, turn back-to-back with your buddy and fin together to the reef staying submerged, and then continue separately very close to the formation until finding a convenient ascent from the scene. And, of course, don't forget to use your camera.

More sharks are found in the southern part of the Gulf but the diver will also meet an occasional solitary specimen in the north. At Ras Muhammed, in open sea, however, you will meet them on almost every dive. **Diving south from Eilat, in fact, provides you with options unknown anywhere else in tropical waters around the world. The Gulf itself provides all the marine flora and fauna of the Indian Ocean ecology without its usual danger, vis-a-vis sharks, while Ras Muhammed can be chosen by the more adventurous.** This index supplies the reader with the 4 most familiar sharks in the Gulf: illustrated, rather than photographed, to give positive and easy identification from any angle.

White-tip Reef Shark *Triaenodan obesus*

Another cmmon species in these waters, primarily a reef dweller not hesitating to enter caves and grottoes and often crossing the reef table into the lagoons.

Black-tip Shark *Carcharinus melanopterus*

One of the most common sharks in the Red Sea and Gulf of Eilat. This nonstop restless open water traveler is frequently seen close to the reefs but not considered dangerous. Always the first to arrive on the scene during or after any unusual underwater disturbance.

Whale Shark *Rhiniodon typus*

This very clumsy and slow cruiser is one of the largest of sharks yet a harmless and peaceful species feeding on plankton, small fish and squid.

Hammerhead Shark *Sphyrna mokarran*

Commonly named for its remarkable head and usually found in open water, but sometimes reaching the reef. A very aggressive predator feeding on fish and crab. Potentially dangerous. The species delivers its young alive in a litter of about 30, each youngster measuring around 40–50 cm (15–20 in) in length.

STONY CORALS

Hexacorallia take the common name of Stony Corals because of their calcium carbonate exoskeleton built by each tiny polyp in the shape of a cup. Over millions of years this tiny creature, in vast communities, has built major landscapes and islands. The scientific name is based upon the fact that Stony Corals possess six arms per-polyp or a multiple thereof. There are about 150 species in the Gulf.

Goniopora sp.

Antipataria sp. Black Coral

Acropora sp.

Gorgonaria sp.

Fungia sp.

FIRE CORAL

Although commonly known as coral, Fire Coral is a Hydroid. It is a major contributor to the topography of the reef and the most common species in the Gulf is *Millepora* with the shape of a burning bush, ochre in color and a distribution along the entire reef ecology. Important: consistant with its common name, Fire Coral produces a poison burning the skin in various degrees of severity depending upon the period of exposure and sensitivity of the skin. Obviously, don't handle it.

SOFT CORALS

Octocorallia, or Soft Corals, do not build an exoskeleton of calcium but support themselves on tiny spines degenerating after death and leaving little trace. They exhibit many beautiful forms and shapes, for example like bushes or fire, and reflect strong colors in pink, red, green, etc. A few do deposit a skeleton of calcium carbonate, such as the Pipe Coral *(Tubipora musica).* They exhibit eight arms or a multiple of that number.

SEA TURTLE

This gentle and easygoing animal is the only reptile to be found in the Gulf of Eilat. Divers are delighted to meet them. These aesthetic and graceful swimmers may reach a length of 1 m. (3.3 ft.) and are usually seen in the southern part of the Gulf. The most common is *Erethmochelis coriacea.* Look for their brownish color and yellow spots and the parasitic Remora usually attached.

Erethmochelis coriacea

OCTOPUS

Octopus sp.

A charming and amusing invertebrate. Unquestionably the master of camouflage among all creatures of the sea. They change not only color but the shape and texture of their bodies to match the environment. Try to discover which stone is the Octopus in the picture below. They also swim with jet power by swallowing water and ejecting it through a special tube. For more leisurely travel they can also crawl on their eight vacuum-cupped legs. The cups are utilized not only for locomotion but to seize their prey. When their camouflage fails the last resort of the Octopus is to eject a cloud of black ink before fleeing from the murky scene.

UNDERWATER PHOTOGRAPHY

Before You Arrive

Virgin reef means virgin territory. In this case the tropical sea off the Sinai desert. So bring your equipment to a favorite photo shop and ask for a thorough check-up and servicing even if your camera has been functioning perfectly.

Heat,dust and high salinity in the Gulf can effect the best cameras when not in top condition. Don't overlook it - do it.

Another equally important pointer for your Red Sea adventure is to bring everything with you: camera, film, flashunit and supply batteries. Israel is a developing country with high duties on imports more than doubling the price of what you may consider a relatively inexpensive and standard replacement. What you seek also may not be readily available. Arrive well stocked for your tour.

For how much to bring follow this simple "rule of thumb" - 1) calculate your average expenditure of film and other equipment during a successful dive for pictures in your own territory, 2) multiply this by the number of dives you are planning in the Gulf, 3) double the figures.

Underwater photography today is still an art, not a science, requiring trial and error. Multiple factors such as camera, color, manufacture of film and speed, light conditions, visibility, and depth are involved. The only computer available to juggle all these factors during a dive is your brain. The **FISH INDEX,** however, is designed with the underwater photographer in mind. It identifies visually, names, and, most important, locates the photographic target for you. Whether hunting for a specific target "on location" or indexing your slides at home after the trip, it is invaluable. Study and read it, and then reread it again before your first dive in the Gulf.

Studio in the Sea

The Gulf of Eilat is a massive, delicate underwater aquarium and the nearest thing to a perfect studio in the sea. The rich invertebrate marine life—soft corals, Gorgonaria, myriads of plankton filter-feeders such as the crinoid(feather stars or sea lillies)- carpet the rocks, reefs and canyons of the Gulf. Meanwhile, on top of this rich wallpaper of life the incredible coral fish of the Red Sea ebb and flow. The place is really an underwater photographer's paradise. There is an extra added attraction too. As the sun retires behind the high mountains of Sinai, between four and five in the afternoon, there is a lengthy period ot twilight when the changeover between day and night in the sea takes place. A transition period when the diver with his camera and flash can capture some of the most exciting moments. Moments such as the mass migration of crinoid to the tops of rock and reef (to catch the accelerated planktonic activity in the night), the leisurely movements of Lion Fish beginning their nocturnal hunt and other species seeking the protection of the corals till dawn. A diver finning carefully, silently, along the reef with camera and flash can capture these brief incredibly beautiful, moments of life.

Camera Care in the Gulf

There are several maintenance problems when diving for pictures in the Gulf. This enclosed stretch of Red Sea combines narrow straits and intense evaporation rates giving the waters a very high salinity. Equipment not maintained, that is, not carefully washed off after a day's dive, tends to disintegrate. The blue corrosive waters of the Gulf, in fact, eat cameras for breakfast. Wash your camera the best way by soaking it in a tub of fresh water with a small amount of liquid detergent added to dissolve the salt build up.

One of the ideal conditions for underwater photography south from Eilat, is the fact that you don't need a boat, apart from certain reefs in the Sharm el-Sheikh area.

Mostly, the fringing reefs are easily accessible from the shore. And that's where delicate photographic equipment takes a beating. The sand of Sinai tends to get in between O-rings while also scratching the lens and dome ports of camera housings.

Perhaps it's needless to say, but remember when you enter the water to take the camera as if it were a delicate baby, submerge it in shallow water, and watch for bubbles. If no bubbles, you can go hunting. If, however, the camera begins leaking on a dive and somehow a sensitive piece of photographic equipment drowns, there is a specific technique for saving it. Immediately, remove the camera and place it in a 50% alcohol solution. Then take it out of the 50% solution and immerse in 100% alcohol. Remove it from the 100% solution and, if you are near civilization, i.e., Willy Halpert's Aqua Sport Diving Centre, place the camera in a freezer until you are ready for the most rapid transfer possible to the nearest camera repair man.(Usually by Arkia Inland Airways to Tel Aviv.) A little bit of salt water tends to turn the most expensive Nikon, Rolleiflex or Hasselblad into something resembling a metal Bouillabaise - within minutes. If you can get the salt water out quickly, this is why alcohol is used, there is a very good chance the camera can be saved. With a Nikonos this fresh water-alcohol treatment combined with a careful blowing out of any moisture, using compressed air from an aqualung, can often produce a complete cure.

Drowned photo equipment causes a strange suicidal tendency in underwater photographers. In fact, those tiny bubbles of escpaing air from an underwater housing can totally ruin a diving vacation. You can prevent this. And that means checking O-rings and camera control seals every evening after a day's diving. Check flash connectors for corrosion also. A good idea is to bring a camera maintenance kit with you: a can of silicone spray, a can of WD-40 or CRC-556, a tube of silicone grease, a tube of silicone cement, a supply of Q-tips, lens tissue, lens cleaning fluid, and a small can of plexiglass polish for those cameras with plexiglass or paraspex front ports. Also include camera parts likely to be expendable, particularly O-rings and control handles.

In the evening, aside from carefully inspecting and cleaning O-ring seals, spray latches and other stainless steel parts with WD-40 and spray flash connectors with the same.

Equipment

The best underwater systems are 35 mm. because of their compact size and the choice of films available for them. Six-by-six cameras, such as Rolleiflex, Rollei 66 and Hasselblad, also produce beautiful and large formal images. However, there is an incredible choice for the lens with a Nikon system. And the Gulf of Eilat offers an incredible choice of subjects: extreme wide-angle vistas, canyons, walls and cliffs, and those extremely small subjects which are the delight of the macro-lens. Every fish photographer finds it necessary at times to use a telephoto lens. With a medium telephoto lens and an extension tube, for example, you can move up and fill the frame with a shy coral dweller.

Ninety-percent of our underwater photography demands supplementry lighting. The diver has two choices: 1) flashbulbs or 2) electronic flash. If a diver opts for flashbulbs and decides to shoot ten rolls of 35 mm. film on his vacation, he will fire off approximately 360 bulbs. (And that's a hell of a lot of flashbulbs to fly in and argue past the Israeli customs). Once bursting into glorious light and life, bulbs are then finished, to be discarded into that bottomless wastebasket, the sea. And, flashbulbs, as we all know, are non-biodegradable, undoubtedly awaiting discovery several centuries later by future historians. As you can deduce, flashbulbs tend to be expensive, bulky and wasteful.

Although more complicated and producing a harsher light, electronic flash systems are less expensive to operate, lighter, and more compact even though their initial cost is higher. (It is a good, although admittedly expensive idea to bring along two flash systems: one serving as a back up unit.) There are several reliable electronic systems that have been on the market for a number of years. One of the best is the Subsea MK 100 manufactured in San Diego, California. It is reliable, compact, and uses a 300 volt battery supplying almost 1,500 flashes. Subsea also makes several other underwater flash units varying in size, output and price.

One of the best 35 mm. Nikon camera systems for electronic flash, i.e., for Nikon F or F2 cameras, is currently made by Oceanic Products in San Leandro, California. There are other very good systems manufactured in Europe. (Diving magazines are your best source for underwater photo equipment information.) The little Nikonos, the only truly underwater camera on the market, is a beautiful versatile system. When photographing with it in the Gulf be sure to bring along extension tubes and closeup lens (again there are many manufacturers). Closeup photography of the corals and the smaller immobile animal life will produce instant art. Studying soft corals in the evening finds all their polyps fully extended and feeding on plankton - excellent subjects for the macro-lens. A bit of flash brings out their beautiful translucency with a range of colors from delicate pink to pulsating purple.

For Personal Comfort

An underwater photographer is a specialized creature. He has to be kept warm, protected and happy in the sea. Good underwater pictures are the result of being able to concentrate on pictures, and only pictures. Being cold, too heavy or too light, or generally dissatisfied with being underwater will under no circumstances generate "great art." So... a few necessary diving items to bring along. Boots. Rubber diving booties with hard soles are invaluable for lumbering across coral tables while carrying aqualung and cameras. The Gulf has a fairly constant temperature range of 21-26°C. (70-80°F) throughout the year even though the coast of Sinai may be boiling or slightly chilly. The water retains its refreshing coolness. But underwater photographers spending considerable time below, mostly watching and waiting, find the water has lost its refreshing cool after the first half hour and it proceeds to become a freezing "bloody cold." A full wet-suit, and the best is with 3/16 in. thickness, is necessary. Any underwater photographer must become deeply involved with his subject to make good pictures, And in doing so he becomes deeply involved with the sea bottom: sea urchins, fire coral, sting rays, scorpion fish, etc. (See **FISH INDEX**). A good pair of diving pants, in fact, prevent your legs from turning into something resembling hamburger. They also, by the way, keep you warm. In the winter, it's a good idea to wear a hood. Gloves, however, become a problem, getting in the way of handling photographic gear. A bouyancy-compensator vest is a must, acting as the photographer's elevator so he can lie on the bottom (after a careful check) or hover in midwater. (A most important thing to remember is to watch how you use your fins. Once stirred up, sand and sediment can ruin your pictures and those of your diving partner.)

Supplies

Bring about twice as much film as you think you will need. Yes, it's *really* that good in the Gulf. A lot of the diving is relatively shallow and you can spend hours in the water if you are so inclined. The best film for 35 mm. is KR 64 (formerly Kodachrome X). Kodachrome is the finest grain, sharpest color film available. Kodachrome 25 (KM 25) is even better than KR 64 because of its finer grain. However KM 25 is a slower film and good only for extreme closeups. The faster KR 64 is ideal for mixed light conditions, i.e., some natural light with some flash. Highspeed

Ektachrome is good for deep water work in natural light but the beauty of this gulf rests on the fact that the most spectacular scenery is generally at shallow depths (less than 20 m. -66 ft.). Within this range there is plenty of natural light because of the excellent visibility and the guaranteed 320 days of extra bright Middle Eastern sun. Kodachrome films are not available for six-by-six cameras and the best alternatives for them are Ektachrome X or Ektachrome Professional. Kodachrome and Ektachrome films are, of course, reversal films producing slides. Slides are to be preferred for underwater photography because they are less expensive and deliver the best picture results. Color negative films, such as Kodacolor, are more expensive because of the cost of individual prints. And the underwater camera enthusiast always makes more mistakes than any other kind of photographer. If you shoot in the sea with a color negative film, you pay for someone to print your mistakes.

With regard to batteries the heat of summer in Sinai tends to sap their power so always bring extras. And remember how batteries, film and other photo supplies in Israel are much more expensive than at home because of high duties on imports. Availability is also a factor. **Bring everything with you.** Remember, also, a good underwater flashlight for twilight and night photography is a must.

Rewards

Is it worth it? Dusk approaches and the sun sinks beyond and behind the mountains of Sinai. Moses Rock near Willy's Aqua Sport comes alive. Fish seek their night places and nocturnal creatures of the sea begin to hunt and feed. The photographer and his partner fin around and between the crevices and fissures of the rock. A darkening sea becomes deep azure blue while a large red nudibranch undulates against this curtain of color. Two yellow-banded butterfly fish peck at the coral polyps for their last meal of the day. A small octopus oozes out of his coral crevice home. Elsewhere, a Lion Fish, striped and moving slowly, spreads his fan-like pectoral fins and imitates the yellow soft coral, camouflaging himself and waiting for his evening meal to pass by. A blue-spotted sting ray sleeps quietly on the sand. The life and color of the Gulf blooms. And the transparent school of glassy sweepers hovering over the rock during the day begins to scatter; these tiny fish seeking their nocturnal hiding places. A photographer's flash makes puddles of white-yellow light against the increasing gloom of the sea.

There are very few places in this world that form such exquisite images — as the Gulf of Eilat.

David Doubilet is well known among the international diving fraternity for his outstanding prize-winning underwater photography and by the international scientific community through his pictorial assignments for National Geographic, including a total of some ten months in the Gulf of Eilat. Inventing a mythical amateur underwater photographer without too much experience, the Editors asked Doubilet to give him an image of photographic possibilities in the Gulf and some professional advice about diving there with camera in hand.

REVIEW & REMINDERS

Why the Diving Tables

Among divers the most common name for nitrogen embolism (formation of dangerous nitrogen bubbles in the body) is "the bends" (see **MEDICINE**)The tables App. 6 were designed to prevent "the bends" after years of scientific research and field tests by the United States Navy, and they are updated periodically as further research continues. Placing these tables in this volume has a twofold purpose: 1) to give you an opportunity to review your knowledge of dive planning with the tables and 2) to make this guide a more useful instrument in your hands at a diving location. Review them carefully. If you have any doubts, difficulty or questions afterwards, seek out the most convenient diving organization in your vicinity and ask for a review of these tables with a qualified instructor. Finding yourself at 40 m. (132 ft.) in "The Canyon" at Dahab is not the time and place to begin a mental review of how to use them.

Terms

Depth: maximum depth reached during the dive whether remaining there for one second or one hour.

Bottom Time: commencement of initial descent until beginning *final* ascent (the period when nitrogen is absorbed into the body).

Decompression Stop(s): a stop made at a specific depth, according to the directions in the tables, permitting excess nitrogen to escape without embolism.

Safe Rate of Ascent: not more than 18 m. (60 ft.) per minute when breathing compressed air (with or without decompression stops).

Total Ascent Time: commencement of *final* ascent until reaching the surface including decompression stops, if any.

Repetitive Dive: any dive within 12 hours of a previous dive.

Interval: the surface time (one atmosphere, between the finish of one dive and the beginning of a repetitive dive.

Repetitive Dive Group: a coefficient, expressed by letters in the tables, indicating the quantity of residual nitrogen remaining in the body after a dive or an interval.

Diving

A bit of information, a little review, and some hints for planning your trip to the Red Sea.

What to Bring

First of all great expectations. They will be realized. First on your list of things to remember, however, should be your diving card certifying diving experience and qualifications. Israeli standards in sport diving are high and the centers in the country are safety conscious. Without your diving card you will find it difficult to rent Scuba gear or obtain air for your cylinders. And the only other alternative will be the added expense of obtaining a medical exam plus undergoing theoretical and practical tests at a local diving center, or hiring a qualified diving guide.

Contrary to popular legend, you do need a wet-suit in the Gulf. Bring your own along because there are few for rental in the Eilat area and the chances of finding your exact size are minimal.

Bring small, light personal diving equipment: regulator, buoyancy-compensator vest, watch, depth gauge, compass, knife, etc. (Remember to pack oil-filled depth gauges in an airtight container for flying.) With regard to regulators a field kit of spares is essential. Because of weight considerations with airlines most divers rent weight belts and cylinders "on location". Equipment rentals from Eilat, by the way, are remarkably inexpensive and you may find it convenient to equip, apart from the smaller personal items, after arrival. Rest assured that if you forget something - it's available.

Air

Clean, safe air is available from compressors checked periodically by the Federation for Underwater Activities in Israel. Certificates to this effect must be displayed in public view. Touring south from

Eilat presents no problems because you can obtain refills at regular intervals from diving centers down the coast
As this volume goes to press the maximum pressures available are 200 atm. (3,000 psi.) but facilities in the Eilat area are being expanded to reach 350 atm. (5,000 psi.) in the not too distant future.

Upon Arrival

Your connecting inland flight to Eilat usually arrives in the afternoon or late afternoon with still time for a dip. The best way to cool off, relax, and limber up a bit is to jump into the water with mask, fins and snorkel. This is important also. Many divers who are not in the water regularly on weekends wisely utilize this day to stretch their muscles, do a bit of skin diving and measure their stamina before planning their first day or two of Scuba. It also provides answers to some basic questions. You discover the high bouyancy in the Gulf of Eilat and calculate how much "lead" you will need. You will already be pleased with the fact that what you read about the richness of marine life in the shallows is true and adjust your dive plans to utilize this blessing (contrary to other locations in the world where divers must seek depth to find variety). Don't forget to bring along your **empty** camera housings for this swim to check for any leaks (you are still near a diving center and have the evening to make repairs before your first dive). Finally, you can practice your stalking techniques and study the light before putting that expensive film into the camera - at a time of day with special benefits for photographers (see PHOTOGRAPHY).

Israelis are famous for their informality and easygoing manner, so don't stand on customary manners if you tend toward formality. The most Continental gentleman usually sheds his tie and uses first names by the second day in Sinai. Feel free to ask questions and strike up conversations with one and all, including the director of the center. You can also request a diving partner and suggest sharing transport costs with local and visiting divers for a particular venture. You will be overwhelmed with a plethora of suggestions about where to stay, where to dive, what to do, and, of course, how to do it. Although this may be considered "bad form" in some parts of the globe, in Israel it's a natural aspect of the social milieu. "When in Rome....".

Don't forget to stow your equipment, well marked with it's owner's name, either under supervision or under lock and key. (This guide recommends that you ask the hotel manager if he might find a storage area under management supervision convenient for your needs - not your hotel room).

Personal Health

Keep in mind that you are diving in a desert climate and dehydrating rapidly both **above** and below water. Because of the low humidity and its resulting comfort, many visitors are totally unaware of this phenomena. Remember to drink more liquids than you feel you need. As a preventive policy add a bit more salt than usual during meals. If you feel a sudden headache coming on, take some salt (not in tablets but table salt dissolved in water or a glass of soda) and you may discover a miraculous cure. Ask for instructions concerning how much water you must take for trips.

Most photographers newly arrived in the region are overwhelmed by the intensity of sunlight in the Middle East - a great contributing factor to good photographic results underwater. Your skin can also be overwhelmed by it. Expose yourself gradually.

Contrary to popular mythology, the sea does not disinfect scratches and abrasions. Develop the habit, immediately after a dive **and** every shower, of applying merchurochrome or merthiolate liberally to prevent those secondary infections nagging along the way.

In and Along the Gulf

Local instructors in this region must, again and again, contend with over enthusiasm engendered by the fantastic visibility in the Gulf of Eilat. (It is, for example, possible to see moonlight at 30 m. (100 ft.) on a night dive). While most divers from overseas have developed an almost unconscious ability to judge their depth by lighting conditions and, secondarily, visibility. So you must consciously discard these habitual presumptions. "Buddy breathing" may be great fun during training but not much fun in the face of necessity. Check your depth gauge frequently to prevent surprises.

Marine flora and fauna in the Red Sea is breathtaking and incredibly distracting, particularly with camera in hand. Check your watch more frequently than usual and make sure you have enough air for those decompression stops.

Israeli medical personnel and facilities, even in Sinai, are of the highest international standards. Israeli organization and "knowhow" guarantees prompt, efficient and extensive medical treatment for diving emergencies regardless of the locality or distances involved. Everything from helicopters to teams of diving doctors are "on call" in the country. **If they get a call**. This depends upon providing yourself with useful information before departing for a dive and upon filing a good plan when not diving in the immediate vicinity of a diving center. The same applies for a trip down the coast with several dives before checking in again at the next center: 1) before departure ask where the nearest emergency, clinical and recompression aid will be available in the area of your dive and 2) file your dive plan(s) in the log at the appropriate diving center including details concerning general area, site of dive(s), number of dives, expected place and time of return (Aqua Sport, Jim's hotel, Manny's restaurant, Joe's Bar, etc., etc.). And remember: without transport immediately available at the site, dives requiring decompression stops are not recommended.

Ecology and Conservation

The marvelous variety and wealth of flora and fauna south from Eilat is the major reason for your diving trip to Israel. Your diving colleagues in Israel want you to enjoy it all again and again, for many years of return adventures. The country's Nature Reserves Authority has defined and set apart nature reserves along the Gulf Coast for just this purpose, sending forth daily patrols to assist, advise, and prevent destruction along these reefs. Each of its centers throughout the country, including Eilat, are marvelous places for obtaining expert information, good regional maps, and life-long friends.

Two pointers in this regard are helpful. Large Wrasse, trigger fish and many other coral species can be easily attracted to a convenient photographic locale with a bit of bread. (Don't forget to ask at your hotel dining room before leaving for a day's dive.) Tapping your knife on a rock can also bring many fish. Secondly, fin along the bottom about I m.(3 ft.) above. This not only avoids harm to flora and fauna but prevents swirling sediment from spoiling good pictures. Taking care when "landing" on bottom not only does the same but helps you avoid passive poisonous-predators or the unwary sting ray (see **FISH INDEX**).

If it's your first time in tropical waters, take note that coral can rip through the thickest wet-suit.

Equipment Care

There is high salinity in the Gulf and it is marvelous for buoyancy, making diving and snorkeling a greater pleasure. For equipment it's another matter. You must rinse diving equipment thoroughly, regulators doubly so, after every dive and not just at the end of the day. On a long trip, take several jerry-cans of fresh water just for this purpose. Corrosion works best on dry salt-caked equipment - and equipment dries rapidly on a desert beach. Read David Doubilet's advice carefully (see **PHOTOGRAPHY**) to protect your photographic equipment. Remember to keep your cylinders out of direct sunlight for extended periods because the Middle Eastern temperatures plus hot metal could blow a safety valve. Sand is a great enemy of both regulators and cameras so remember to transport them in proper cases or a nylon bag. Cylinders also, should be stacked carefully on vehicles with padding between them and their valves well protected.

Good To Remember

A small nitrogen residual will make a big difference on a deep dive.
A large nitrogen residual will make little difference on a shallow dive.
If more than one dive in the day, make your deep dive first.
Tables have no safety margin whatsoever: make an unlisted and unrequired decompression stop at 3 m. (10 ft.) for three minutes on all dives to 12 m. (40 ft.) or more.

Unless you rate the equivalent of a "Three Star" CMAS diver ("Second Class" in England, "Advanced" in America, and formerly "Second Echelon" in France), dives requiring decompression stops are not recommended.

The smallest visible air bubble ascends at about 18 m. (60 ft.) per minute: let all your bubbles climb faster than yourself and you won't exceed the "safe rate of ascent."

Within 24 hours after any dive do not climb to an altitude of more than 700 m. (2,300 ft.) above sea level whether by plane, train, car or foot-power. (Take the last day off before your flight home to enjoy the snorkeling and the sun on the beach).

Read the **FISH INDEX** again before your first dive in the Gulf.

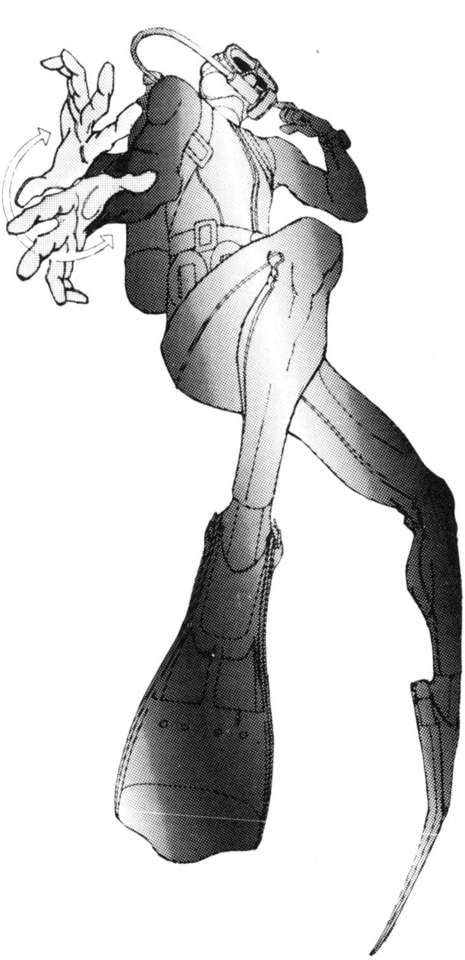

SOMETHING WRONG
(point out)

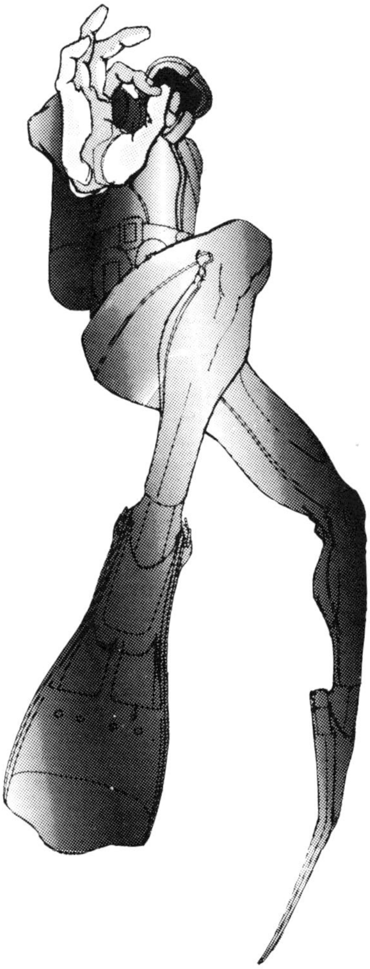

EVERYTHING O.K.
(answer or question)

DANGEROUS
(followed by indication)

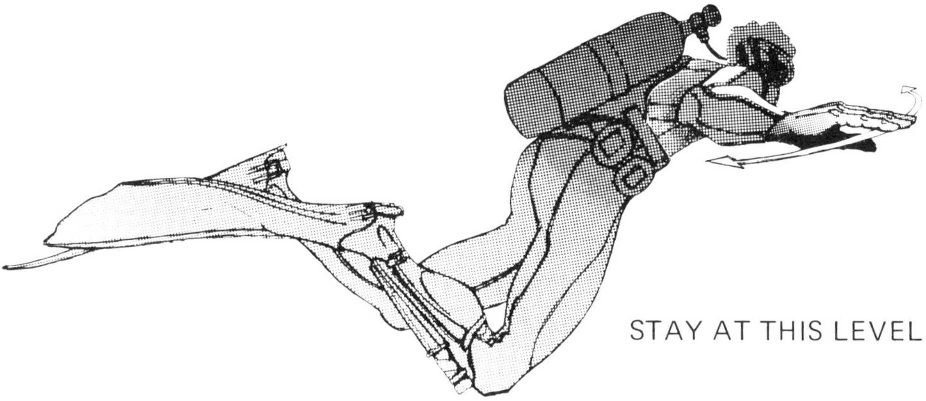

STAY AT THIS LEVEL

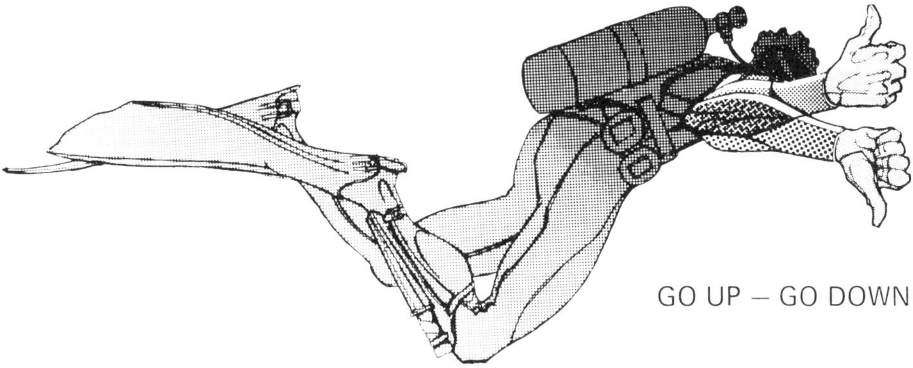

GO UP – GO DOWN

GO THIS DIRECTION

STOP DON'T MOVE

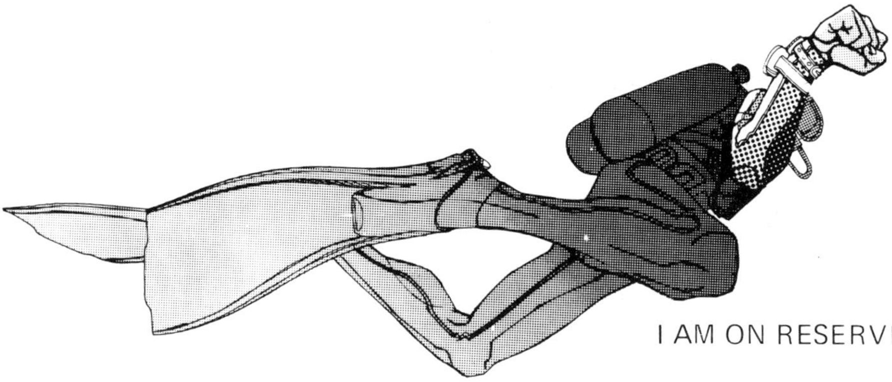

I AM ON RESERVE

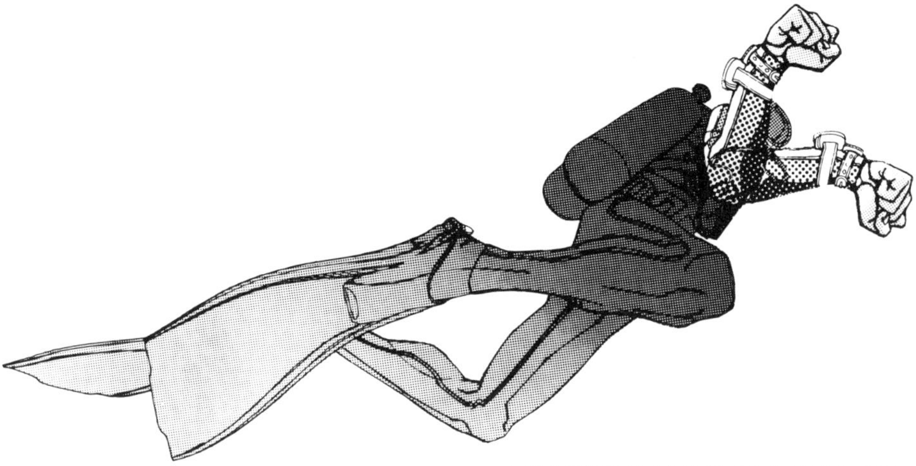

I CANNOT OPEN MY RESERVE
(please open it)

I HAVE NO AIR
(need buddy breathing)

FOR DECOMPRESSION STOPS GIVE "STAY AT THIS LEVEL" AND THEN POINT TO WATCH AND DEPTH GAUGE.

MEDICINE

The following review is not designed for instruction but to refresh your memory for an emergency at a diving location. The sections marked **PREVENTION** also provide a review of some basic diving rules.

EAR PAIN

Cause: not equalizing air pressure between the outer and middle ear because of a blocked or constricted Eustachian tube.

Signs: pain, loss of equilibrium, loss in hearing, dizziness and nausea, internal and/or external bleeding, broken ear drum.

Treatment: stop the dive if you can't equalize. If there is a loss of equilibrium stay calm, and remain in place. Hold on to something and wait for three minutes, in order to equalize temperatures. Then make a controlled ascent, holding onto your buddy. See a medical specialist if there is bleeding, and discontinue diving until a doctor certifies a complete recovery.

Prevention: always equalize ear pressure as you dive (and if you don't succeed — STOP THE DIVE) and do not dive with a cold blocked sinuses, or blocked Eustachian tube.

REVERSED EAR

Cause: increased pressure in the Eustachian tube without equalization in the outer passage because of tight fitting hood, earplugs, etc.

Signs: extreme pain, external bleeding, broken ear drum.

Treatment: stop bleeding with sterile gauze and see a doctor as soon as possible.

Prevention: use a diving hood vented at the ears and don't dive with ear plugs.

SQUEEZE

Cause: sudden unequal outside pressure, from a rapid descent, on a closed air space such as lungs, ears, sinuses, face mask and suit.

Signs: pain and hemorrhage in the eyes, sinus pain, nosebleeds, swollen or bruised face, sudden chest pain.

Treatment: stop the dive, treat for shock in extreme cases and stop any bleeding.

Prevention: equalize pressure in all air spaces when descending, release air from your nose into your mask during descent. Use a properly fitted mask.

HYPERVENTILATION SYNDROME

Cause: poor physical condition, fatigue, inadequate training, fear, panic, chilling: all resulting in rapid breathing.

Signs: 1) underwater — unending stream of too many bubbles and any observable symptoms. 2) surface — anxiety, panic, very rapid breathing, loss of self-control, numbness in the hands and feet and their muscular contraction in extreme cases.

Treatment: 1) underwater — stop all physical exertion and rest where you are, breathe easy and terminate the dive with a controlled ascent; 2) surface — inflate your vest and rest without exertion, breathe slowly and deeply until signs disappear, seek professional treatment in extreme cases.

Prevention: **proper physical condition, avoid over exertion, control your dive and your breathing.**

CARBON DIOXIDE POISONING

Cause: dirty air, regulator hose or snorkel tube too long, creating excess "dead volume", rapid and shallow breathing, over exertion, improper breathing, holding breath while diving.

Signs: panting, dizziness, nausea, headache, anxiety, fear, panic, heart palpitation, general distress, loss of consciousness.

Treatment: stop the dive immediately and make a controlled ascent with your partner and rest on the surface, breathe fresh air slowly and deeply and, if necessary, take oxygen.

Prevention: **check your equipment and your air before a dive, check compressors at refill stations, learn correct breathing for Scuba.**

CARBON MONOXIDE POISONING

Cause: dirty air in diving cylinders because of inefficient compressors or compressor air-intake near sources of pollution (particularly petrol).

Signs: anoxia, breathlessness on exertion, impaired vision, dizziness, ringing in the ears, vertigo, headache, nausea, cherry-red skin, tongue and lip coloration, heart palpitation: all appearing swiftly before unconsciousness, loss of consciousness.

Treatment: stop the dive immediately at the first signs, ascend and breathe fresh air, give oxygen or artificial respiration if necessary, seek medical advice in extreme cases.

Prevention: **check the compressors where you seek cylinder refills, particularly note proximity of exhaust and intake systems, and check the proximity of traffic and other sources of pollution.**

OXYGEN POISONING

Cause: breathing compressed air at 90 m. (300 ft.) depth or more, that is, when the partial pressure of oxygen reaches 2 atms. or more.

Signs: twitching and trembling of the skin, tongue and lips, muscle spasm, vertigo, dizziness, nausea, muscle contraction, convulsion, loss of consciousness.

Treatment: stop the dive immediately, ascend and breathe fresh air, let any convulsions disappear naturally without constricting the patient, use a convenient mouthpiece to prevent tongue biting, medical supervision for not less than 12 hours.

Prevention: **never use closed-circuit oxygen apparatus beyond a depth of 8 m. (26 ft.), and do not dive beyond 40-50 m. (125-155 ft.) with ordinary compressed air. (for 3 star divers C.M.A.S. only).**

AIR EMBOLISM

Cause: lungs rupturing because of failure to expire during ascent with Scuba or failure to vent air properly during free ascent after ditching Scuba.

Signs: chest pains, pneumothorax, paralysis, breathing with the rib cage instead of the diaphragm, sharp pain on inhalation, shortness of breath, blood froth at the mouth and lips, blindness, headache, stomach pain with or without vomiting, subcutaneous ephysema on the skin of the neck, shock, collapse, loss of consciousness (various paralyses depend upon point of injury in the brain).

Treatment: **immediate!** transport to a recompression chamber under medical supervision, meanwhile place the patient in a comfortable horizontal position, keep warm, give oxygen in extreme cases, do not give narcotics or tranquilizers.

Prevention: **breathe normally during ascent with Scuba and vent air properly until surfacing on free ascent.**

VOMITING

Cause: air polluted with oil, too much food in the stomach, indigestion.

Signs: Sickness and nausea.

Treatment: stop the dive at the first signs of not feeling well and if you must vomit underwater take out the regulator to prevent consequent strangling, if a patient is strangling at the surface apply artificial respiration.

Prevention: **check your compressors at refill stations, check your air before a dive, don't eat too much before a dive don't drink carbonated beverages before a dive, and — obviously — don't dive when not feeling well.**

DROWNING

Cause: water in the lungs or contracting the throat (laryngo spasm) stops respiration.

Signs: unconsciousness, pale skin, blue lips and finger tips, failure of respiration, white froth at the mouth.

Treatment: immediate artificial respiration (see ARTIFICIAL RESPIRATION), if no heart beat alternate with external heart massage, call a doctor, continue until patient is breathing independently, insist on an immediate medical examination.

EXPOSURE TO COLD

Cause: diving without a wet suit for prolonged periods or fatigue.

Signs: chilling, trembling, constricted blood vessels, pale skin, indifference to the surroundings, loss of self-control, loss of consciousness.

Treatment: dry and warm the patient, cover and protect from the wind, transport to a warm place, give hot drinks (not alcohol), a hot bath or shower at 42°C in extreme cases under medical supervision.

Prevention: **stop before chilling begins.**

NARCOSIS

Cause: when an inert gas under partial pressure, such as nitrogen, acts upon the nervous system like a narcotic: the onset of symptoms are individual. Contributing factors include depth and duration of dive, experience, physical condition and psychology of the diver.

Signs: drunkeness, slow thinking and clumsiness, inability to concentrate, metallic taste in the mouth and tickling sensation in the lips, a feeling of warmth and comfort, euphoria, irrational behavior that may lead to fatality.

Treatment: level off and hold the dive at the onset of signs and as a partner in extreme cases remain cool, control the situation, seize the patient from behind using water rescue training techniques, return to the surface with all the necessary decompression stops.

Prevention: **narcosis can begin at 40 m. (130 ft.), but has been known to happen at lesser depths, therefore international sport diving standards do not recommend diving beyond 40 m. Important: have a good night's sleep before a deep dive. Never attempt to make a deep dive as a "first" dive, after a prolonged period of not diving. When planning a deep dive, to save bottom time, descend as quickly as you can only to a depth of 25 m. (75 ft.). From this point continue to descend slowly, in order to avoid acute onset of nitrogen narcosis. Experience and physical condition are vital factors to consider before attempting a deep dive — go with an experienced and familiar partner, do not drink alcohol before any deep dive, women should not attempt a deep dive during menstruation, don't take tranquilizers, cold pills, etc., before diving.**

DECOMPRESSION SICKNESS ("Bends")

Cause: nitrogen bubbles develop in the body during an uncontrolled and incorrect ascent, i.e., without the guidance of decompression diving tables.

Signs: 1) itching and discoloration of the skin, pain in the joints but otherwise the diver feels well; 2) extreme pain in the joints, breathing difficulty, pain and pressure in the chest, headache, impaired vision, weakness or paralysis, tingling and numbness in the limbs. stomach pain with or without vomiting, shock, collapse, loss of consciousness.

Treatment: remove the patient to a recompression chamber under medical supervision, transport with a minimum of motion and jarring, cover for warmth, provide oxygen if necessary, do not give narcotics or tranquilizers.

Prevention: **plan your dives exactly within the decompression tables and maintain the plan during the dive. Do not exceed the "safe rate of ascent" (see page 176), do not fly within 24 hours of a dive, do not climb higher than 300 m. (990 ft.) above sea level within 12 hours of a dive.**

UNCONSCIOUSNESS (UNDERWATER)

Cause: various accidents may cause loss of consciousness during a dive.

Treatment: **it is crucial that the diving partner keep calm:** bring the patient to the surface as quickly as possible, **with a proper emergency ascent.** Any equipment manipulation necessary will be done on the victim, for example dropping **his** weight belt, inflating **his** vest if needed etc. While constantly making sure he is venting excess air pressure in the lungs, release all encumbering and weighty equipment at the surface and begin artificial respiration immediately during the tow, continue on shore and give heart massage if necessary.

UNCONSCIOUSNESS (ON SHORE)

1. Take off mask and regulator and loosen all constrictive gear and clothing.
2. Keep all equipment to be later checked for malfunction and detailed investigation.
3. Give artificial respiration and cardiac massage, if necessary, until patient is breathing independently, meanwhile call a doctor, and insist on an **immediate** medical examination even if the patient quickly recovers consciousness.
4. When calling for a doctor specify, if possible, the nature of the emergency so the medical facility can prepare and/or dispatch specialists, recompression chamber, staff, etc.
5. Place the patient in the "coma position" if necessary.
6. Protect the patient carefully during convulsion.
7. Internal bleeding — immediate medical supervision is absolutely necessary so transport either doctor or patient, whichever is more advisable, while reducing movement and jarring to the minimum possible under the circumstances.
8. External bleeding — stop with sterile bandages and/or pressure at the proper points in the proper manner.

CARE OF THE PATIENT

1. Give artificial respiration and cardiac massage if necessary.
2. Provide qualified medical supervision as quickly as possible.
3. Take off mask and regulator and loosen all constrictive gear and clothing.
4. Place the patient in a comfortable horizontal position.
5. Keep all equipment to be later checked for malfunction and detailed investigation.

6. Protect the patient carefully during convulsion.
7. Keep the patient motionless if there are signs of internal bleeding.
8. Stop external bleeding with sterile bandages and proper pressure.

ARTIFICIAL RESPIRATION

E.A.R. — Expired Air Respiration

1. Begin immediately even on the surface.
2. Be sure the air passage is not blocked and the patient's head is in the correct position: pull the head back and the jaw down with the tongue unblocked.
3. When applying respiration through the nose, close the mouth by gripping the jaw and closing the mouth with the thumb.
4. Blow strongly (through the mouth or nose) while checking to see the chest is inflating.
5. Let the chest deflate naturally by itself.
6. Repeat at a rate of 12-14 cycles per minute.
7. Continue until the patient is breathing independently or a doctor arrives.

EXTERNAL CARDIAC MASSAGE

1. Use immediately when you **suspect** there is no heart function: no pulse and no heartbeat, check both.
2. Place the patient on his back on a hard surface.
3. Find the pressure point in the lower 2/3 of the sternum.
4. Push strongly every second for six seconds and then immediately follow with one cycle of E.A.R., followed again by massage, etc.
5. Continue the alternate sequence until heart function is restored or a doctor arrives.
6. IMPORTANT: INCORRECT MASSAGE CAN BE DANGEROUS AND HARMFUL, WHILE CORRECT MASSAGE AND E.A.R. MAY SAVE LIFE.

APPENDICES

THE FEDERATION FOR UNDERWATER ACTIVITIES IN ISRAEL - FUAI

P.O. Box 6110 Tel Aviv 61060, Tel: (03) 457432.

The Federation was founded in 1966 by a handful of diving-crazy pioneers, headed by the late General Abraham Yoffe (Res.), President of the Nature Reserves Authority. From these small beginnings the Federation has made astonishing progress. By the end of 1987, it had certified some 20 000 divers.

The Federation is a non-profit organization recognized by the Israel Sports Authority of the Ministry of Education and Culture. The Federation is affiliated to the International Diving Association CMAS, and also has close ties with other organizations such as the BSAC, PADI, NAUI and, naturally, with our colleagues of the Egyptian Diving Association.

The Federation operates within the framework of the "Law of Sport Diving" passed in the Knesset (Israel's parliament) in 1980. This legislation defines elementary safety rules and lays down criteria for the qualification of divers at various levels. Its standards for operating diving clubs and diving schools are particularly stringent. Consequently, the different courses and services offered are of the highest standard.

The Federation has three main institutions:

A. The Executive Committee

This is a body which numbers 12 members and is elected once every two years by all those who hold valid membership. It represents the diving community, determines and implements policy and is responsible for the functioning of the entire body. Yoram Ziv is the present chairman of the Federation.

B. The Federation's Committees

The Federation has three professional committees: the training committee chaired by Willy Halpert, the medical committee chaired by Dr Shraga Wexler, and the tourism committee chaired by Ruthie Schilling. These committees are in charge of establishing professional standards and supervising implementation in their various specialized fields.

C. The Federation's Secretariat

The secretariat comprises a coordinator/director general and a secretary. The secretariat is an executive body, responsible for all aspects of the Federation's functioning. The coordinator, who is nominated by the management, also serves as the chief inspector keeping a close watch on the equipment and services offered by the diving centers, and ensuring that courses meet the high standards set. The present director general is Rubi Eviatar.

Each diving center is operated in accordance with the government's diving legislation and supplies services to holders of valid diver's certificates who hold the current compulsory insurance required. All diving organizations affiliated to CMAS as well as to American diving associations are recognised. Foreign divers are reminded that they, too, are required to hold the special local Israeli diving insurance available from the diving centers or the Federation. The insurance, which costs about $7, is valid for a year and covers the diver against diving accidents to a maximum value of $6000. It includes evacuation, treatment in a recompression chamber and hospitalization. The insurance is valid within Israeli territorial waters and in Sinai. The insurance agency handling the policy is A. Rafael Insurance Company Ltd., Tel: (03)-621785, 615685.

Recompression Chambers

In the Haifa area: Hyperbaric Institute Tel: (04)-513563, 523577. In the Eilat area: Yoseftal Hospital - Tel: (059)73151-5. In the event of an accident, the rescue teams of the diving centers, which are equipped with resuscitation facilities, should be used, and a Magen David Adom ambulance ordered.

DIVING CENTERS IN ISRAEL

SNAPIR

Tel Aviv Port, Tel: (03) 450366, 450995, Telex: 341781.
Manager: Nachum Sela.
20 Complete SCUBA sets, Mediterranean diving tours, Sinai diving safaris, 2 and 3 star courses. SNAPIR imports Scubapro equipment to Israel and are agents for BAUER compressors.

OCTOPUS

Tel Aviv Marina, Tel: (03) 282400, 295440.
Managers: Arik Rinkov, Ronnie Fishman.
35 Complete SCUBA sets, 2 boats, Mediterranean diving tours, Sinai diving safaris, equipment sale.

ACHZIV

P.O. Box 404, Naharia, Tel: (04) 823671.
Manager: Danny Birenbaum.
30 Complete SCUBA sets, 2 boats, guided dives in the northern area, cave diving, Sinai diving safaris, courses at all levels.

NAHARIA

4 Ha'izdarechet St. Naharia, Tel: (04) 926609.
Manager: Gidon Shapira.
20 Complete SCUBA sets, diving tours in the north, Eilat and the Sinai, 1 boat, 2 and 3 star courses.

RAMY DIVING CENTER

P.O. Box 3289 Akko, Tel: (04) 918990.
Manager: Ramy Sadnai.
20 Complete SCUBA sets, boats - 2 large, one small, diving -Akko and Eilat areas. courses at all levels.

CAESAREA

Ma'agan Caesarea, P.O. Box 1211 Caesarea, Tel: (063) 61787, 61441.
Manager: Yitzchak Asher.
20 Complete SCUBA sets, boat dives in Herod's ancient harbour, underwater fishing, diving courses.

SHIKMONA

Ma'agan Sport Hakishon, Tel: (04) 710482, 662005.
Manager: Shlomo Levi.
Boat diving -daily excursions, 20 complete SCUBA sets, diving courses, underwater fishing, cruises to Akko.

AQUASPORT INTERNATIONAL RED SEA DIVING CENTER LTD.

Coral Beach P.O. Box 300 Eilat 88102, Tel: (059) 72788, Telex 7752 AQUAS IL. Director: Willie Halpert.
Manager: Nir Avni.
120 Complete SCUBA sets, boat and land diving excursions in Eilat, Sinai diving safaris, sale of equipment - sole importers of SEATEC, POSEIDON, SOS and distributors of all major brands, underwater photography, restaurant, divers' hostel, courses at all levels.

LUCKY DIVERS

Moriah Hotel Eilat 88000, Tel: (059) 75749, 71057, 72151, Telex 7761 TRET.
Director: Ami Ben Tzvi. Manager: Gidi Shamir.
40 Complete SCUBA sets, diving in the Eilat area, diving from the yacht Sue-Ellen, Sinai diving safaris, courses at all levels, importers of IST, BEAVER, SEAQUEST equipment.

MANTA

Red Sea Sports Club, Caravan Hotel, Coral Beach, Tel: (059) 76569.
Manager: Shmulik Mashiach.
50 Complete SCUBA sets, daily excursions on the yacht Andromeda, diving in Eilat and Sinai diving safaris, courses at all levels.

RED SEA SPORTS CLUB

King's Wharf, King Solomon's Palace Hotel, North Beach Eilat, Tel: (059) 79685, Telex 7765.
Manager: Tzvi Agadi.50 Complete SCUBA sets, boat excursions, Eilat and Sinai diving safaris, diving courses at all levels, equipment sale, underwater photography school.

SEACLAUDE

Aviya Sonesta Hotel Eilat, Tel: (059)79222, 72825, Telex 7764.
Managers: Vicki and Claude Oppenheim.
20 Complete SCUBA sets, specialists in introductory dives, diving courses.

DIVING BOATS

FANTASEA CRUISES

P.O. Box 420 Herzlia B., Tel: (053) 666482, 663555, Telex: 35770 COIN IL attn DIVERS.

Manager: Howard Rosenstein. Captain: Yehuda Reich.

12 Passengers, cruises along the Sinai and Eilat coasts.

SUE-ELLEN

Lucky Divers, Tel: (059) 73876, Telex: 7761 TRET.

Manager: Ami Ben Tzvi.

Cruises to Coral Island and along the shores of the Sinai. Daily excursions -55 passengers, cruises - 12 passengers.

SUN BOAT

Aquamarine Ltd. Club Ashkelon 78475, Tel: (051) 36733/4/5/6, Telex: 25414.

Resort Manager: Harry Lonai. Captain: Yishai Vaknin.

Charters and cruises along Sinai coast, 12 berths including 6 double cabins with facilities.

WINDSURFING

Nature has been generous to this part of the world, making the exciting sport of windsurfing possible on all levels. The hot air trapped between the mountain sides of Jordan and Israel rushes through the desert to its final destination - Eilat. Consequently, north winds blow here most of the year, averaging 3 - 6 Bft.

If you are keen to learn windsurfing during your stay, the lagoon in front of the King Solomon's Palace Hotel is the ideal place for it. The lagoon is calm and sheltered from excess wind, factors which enable you to master the basic manoeuvres of windsurfing in only 4 hours! Falling in is part of the game in the beginning, but who does not enjoy the refreshing water of the Red Sea? If you are past the absolute beginner's stage, and have reached an intermediate level, you will find Eilat's North Beach rewarding, both in terms of equipment available and windsurfing conditions - even if you are only a holiday surfer keeping up to date with the latest developments by reading the back of your cornflakes packet every morning!

The range of boards available on the North Beach includes -

Beginners: Hifly 300, Mistral Kahlua, Tiga.

Intermediate surfers: Gal 360, Vinta 340-370, Klepper 340.

Advanced surfers: Klepper 295-320, Gal 265-295-320.

Sails are available from 3 sqm - 6sqm, fully battened.

Before surfing, inform yourself through the local surf instructors about the border restrictions and the offshore wind. The further out you get, the more it increases in strength. A rescue boat is available to ensure the safety of all surfers.

Flat, very salty water and high winds give your board extra buoyancy - the perfect mix for all speed freaks. At the North Beach, you can challenge ski boats and cut the Red Sea to pieces with splashy gybes...proving that the biblical Moses and the modern windsurfer do have a common denominator! The low humidity (don't forget that you are in the desert) will bring you back to the beach after a while for refreshments. The Neviot 82 Bar/Restaurant offers an uncomplicated menu with the right amount of calories, good music and a private beach with deck chairs where your beloved one (or ones) can admire your ever improving surf skills. A Sailing Center renting dinghies and catamarans is also located on the North Beach, and is the only one of its kind in town. If you are really into gybing, experience the ultimate gybe orgy - an 8km windsurfing safari from the North Beach to the Coral Beach, downwind all the way!

At the Coral Beach you can meet the local surf matadors who will be only too happy to explain and show off the newest and craziest manoeuvres in vogue for the moment. Strong side-shore winds and 1-1.5m chop makes this location the favorite hangout for advanced surfers. As the name Coral Beach suggests, you have to watch out for your equipment, as well as your feet. Unless you have a masters degree from your correspondence course in hot charcoal dancing, it is advisable to wear shoes! Do not forget your rented equipment lying on the rocky beach, otherwise the surf instructors' pent-up tensions are likely to be vented on you! Boards available are: The Fanatic Funboard line and the Gal epoxy line 265-295-320-360, all with fully battened sails.

Favorite joints for keeping your calorie level above zero are the Caravan Rondo Bar and the Aqua Sport Pub, all located within 60 meters of the spot where your jumpgybes and 360's are making history! These hangouts are also well frequented at night with surfers using salt water as after shave, and producing plenty of spinouts after a couple of Maccabees - the well-liked local beer. And, finally, some encouraging facts about the temperatures in Eilat:
Average air temperature: May - September: 35 - 40 degrees centigrade, October - April: 28 - 34 degrees.
Average water temperature: May - September 25 - 26 degrees, October -April: 21 - 22 degrees.

WINDSURFING IN THE SINAI — DAHAB

The area of Dahab offers the best windsurfing in the entire region of the Sinai, with two chief launching spots:

DIZAHAV

Windsurfing in the area of Dizahav is side shore. In the lagoon formed between the eastern reef and the bay, the sea is very still but the wind is very strong — over 25 knots.

DAHAB

Surfing is offshore. Inside the protected area formed by the reef, the water is still but winds are strong. Once you venture out beyond the line of the reef to the east, the sea is more turbulent but without breakers, and the wind is exceptionally strong — over 25-30 knots.

IMPORTANT

* Be very careful not to drift toward the southern reef, and not to approach the area alongside the northern reef.

* Be wary about leaving the protected area formed by the reef, as the winds here are very strong and you have to contend with open sea conditions.

* No facilities exist to buy equipment, or to replace broken equipment. Bring all equipment with you from Israel.

* AS YOU CANNOT RELY ON ASSISTANCE FROM THE BEACH IF YOU DO HAPPEN TO DRIFT OUT, YOU SHOULD BE EXTRA CAREFUL!!

Shalom and looking forward to carving gybes with you in Eilat!
ANDY USELIUS

APPENDIX No. 2
TEMPERATURES AND HUMIDITY IN EILAT

	Temperatures				
	Average maximum		Average minimum		Average daily humidity
	°C	°F	°C	°F	
January	20.9	70	10.1	50	50
February	22.5	72.5	11.1	52	48
March	25.8	77	13.7	55	40
April	30.7	86	17.9	62	35
May	35.5	95	22.2	72	34
June	38.3	100	23.8	74	29
July	39.8	103	26.1	79	28
August	40.2	104	26.5	79.5	30
September	37.3	99	24.8	75	37
October	33.2	92	21.2	70	42
November	27.6	81	16.3	61	45
December	22.4	72	11.4	52	49

APPENDIX No. 3
CONVERSION TABLES FOR KM. & MI. M. & YDS.

kilometers		miles	meters		yards
1.609	**1**	0.621	0.914	**1**	1.094
3.219	**2**	1.243	1.829	**2**	2.187
4.828	**3**	1.864	2.743	**3**	3.281
6.437	**4**	2.485	3.658	**4**	4.374
8.047	**5**	3.107	4.572	**5**	5.468
9.656	**6**	3.728	5.486	**6**	6.562
11.266	**7**	4.350	6.401	**7**	7.655
12.875	**8**	4.971	7.315	**8**	8.749
14.484	**9**	5.592	8.230	**9**	9.843
16.094	**10**	6.214	9.144	**10**	10.936
32.187	**20**	12.427	18.288	**20**	21.872
48.281	**30**	18.641	27.432	**30**	32.808
64.375	**40**	24.855	36.576	**40**	43.745
80.468	**50**	31.068	45.720	**50**	54.681

APPENDIX No. 4
CONVERSION TABLES FOR FEET, METERS & FATHOMS

Feet	*Fathoms*	*Meters*	*Feet*	*Fathoms*	*Meters*
1	—	0.3048	59.1	9.8	**18**
1½	¼	0.4572	**60**	**10**	18.3
2	—	0.6096	62.3	10.4	**19**
3	½	0.9144	65.6	10.9	**20**
3.2808	0.5486	**1**	**70**	11.7	21.3
4	—	1.2192	**80**	13.3	24.4
4½	¾	1.3716	**90**	**15**	27.4
5	—	1.5240			
6	**1**	1.8288	98.4	16.4	**30**
6.5616	1.0936	**2**	**100**	16.7	30.5
7	—	2.1336	**120**	**20**	36.6
8	—	2.4384	131.2	21.9	**40**
9	**1½**	2.7432	164.0	27.3	**50**
9.8424	1.6304	**3**	**180**	**30**	54.9
10	—	3.048	196.8	32.8	**60**
12	**2**	3.7	**200**	33.3	61.0
13.1	2.2	**4**	229.7	38.3	**70**
16.4	2.7	**5**	**240**	**40**	73.2
18	**3**	5.5	262.5	43.7	**80**
19.6	3.3	**6**	295.3	49.2	**90**
20	3.3	6.1	**300**	**50**	91.5
23.0	3.8	**7**	328.1	54.7	**100**
24	**4**	7.3	**360**	**60**	109.8
26.2	4.4	**8**	360.9	60.1	**110**
29.5	4.9	**9**	393.7	65.6	**120**
30	**5**	9.1	**400**	66.7	121.9
32.8	5.5	**10**	**420**	**70**	128.1
36	**6**	**11**	426.5	71.1	**130**
39.4	6.6	**12**	459.3	76.6	**140**
40	6.7	12.2	**480**	**80**	146.4
42	7	12.8	492.1	82.0	**150**
42.7	7.1	**13**	**500**	83.3	152.4
45.9	7.7	**14**	524.9	87.5	**160**
48	**8**	14.6	**540**	**90**	164.7
49.2	8.2	**15**	557.7	93.0	**170**
50	8.3	15.2	590.5	98.4	**180**
52.5	8.7	**16**	**600**	**100**	183.0
54	**9**	16.5	623.4	103.9	**190**
55.8	9.3	**17**	656.2	109.4	**200**

APPENDIX No. 5
STANDARD AIR DECOMPRESSION TABLES

TABLE 1: STANDARD AIR DECOMPRESSION TABLES 1970

DEPTH (FEET)	BOTTOM (TIME) (MM)	TIME TO FIRST STOP (MIN : SEC)	DECOMPRESSION STOPS					TOTAL ASCENT (MIN : SEC)	REPETITIVE GROUP
			M. 15 FT. 50	12 40	9 30	6 20	3 10		
12	200	–					0	0:40	*
M.	210	0:30					2	2:40	N
	230	0:30					7	7:40	N
	250	0:30					11	11:40	O
FT.	270	0:30					15	15:40	O
40	300	0:30					19	19:40	Z
15	100	–					0	0:50	*
M.	110	0:40					3	3:50	L
	120	0:40					5	5:50	M
	140	0:40					10	10:50	M
	160	0:40					21	21:50	N
	180	0:40					29	29:50	O
	200	0:40					35	35:50	O
FT.	220	0:40					40	40:50	Z
50	240	0:40					47	47:50	Z
18	60	–					0	1:00	*
M.	70	0:50					2	3:00	K
	80	0:50					7	8:00	L
	100	0:50					14	15:00	M
	120	0:50					26	27:00	N
	140	0:50					39	40:00	O
	160	0:50					48	49:00	Z
FT.	180	0:50					56	57:00	Z
60	200	0:40				1	69	71:00	Z
21	50	–					0	1:10	*
M.	60	1:00					8	9:10	K
	70	1:00					14	15:10	L
	80	1:00					18	19:10	M
	90	1:00					23	24:10	N
	100	1:00					33	34:10	N
	110	0:50				2	41	44:10	O
	120	0:50				4	47	52:10	O
	130	0:50				6	52	59:10	O
	140	0:50				8	56	65:10	Z
	150	0:50				9	61	71:10	Z
FT.	160	0:50				13	72	86:10	Z
70	170	0:50				19	79	99:10	Z
24	40	–					0	1:20	*
M.	50	1:10					10	11:20	K
	60	1:10					17	18:20	L
	70	1:10					23	24:20	M
	80	1:00				2	31	34:20	N
	90	1:00				7	39	47:20	N
	100	1:00				11	46	58:20	O
	110	1:00				13	53	67:20	O
	120	1:00				17	56	74:20	Z
	130	1:00				19	63	83:20	Z
FT.	140	1:00				26	69	96:20	Z
80	150	1:00				32	77	110:20	Z
27	30	–					0	1:30	*
M.	40	1:20					7	8:30	J
	50	1:20					18	19:30	L
	60	1:20					25	26:30	M
	70	1:10				7	30	38:30	N
	80	1:10				13	40	54:30	N
	90	1:10				18	48	67:30	O
	100	1:10				21	54	76:30	Z
	110	1:10				24	61	86:30	Z
FT.	90	1:00				32	68	101:30	Z
	130	1:00			5	36	74	116:30	Z
30	25	–					0	1:40	*
M.	30	1:30					3	4:40	I
	40	1:30					15	16:40	K
	50	1:20				2	24	27:40	L
	60	1:20				9	28	38:40	N
	70	1:20				17	39	57:40	O
	80	1:20				23	48	72:40	O
	90	1:10			3	23	57	84:40	Z
	100	1:10			7	23	66	97:40	Z
FT.	110	1:10			10	34	72	117:40	Z
100	120	1:10			12	41	78	132:40	Z
33	20	–					0	1:50	*
M.	25	1:40					3	4:50	H
	30	1:40					7	8:50	J
	40	1:30				2	21	24:50	L
	50	1:30				8	26	35:50	M
	60	1:30				18	36	55:50	N
	70	1:20			1	23	48	73:50	O
	80	1:20			7	23	57	88:50	Z
FT.	90	1:20			12	30	64	107:50	Z
110	100	1:20			15	37	72	125:50	Z

TABLE 1: STANDARD AIR DECOMPRESSION TABLES 1970

DEPTH (FEET)	BOTTOM (TIME) (MM)	TIME TO FIRST STOP (MIN : SEC)	DECOMPRESSION STOPS M. 15 FT. 50	12 40	9 30	6 20	3 10	TOTAL ASCENT (MIN : SEC)	REPETI-TIVE GROUP
36	15	–					0	2:00	*
M.	20	1:50					2	4:00	H
	25	1:50					6	8:00	I
	30	1:50					14	16:00	J
	40	1:40				5	25	32:00	L
	50	1:40				15	31	48:00	N
	60	1:30			2	22	45	71:00	O
	70	1:30			9	23	55	89:00	O
	80	1:30			15	27	63	107:00	Z
FT.	90	1:30			19	37	74	132:00	Z
120	100	1:30			23	45	80	150:00	Z
39	10	–					0	2:10	*
M.	15	2:00					1	3:10	F
	20	2:00					4	6:10	H
	25	2:00					10	12:10	J
	30	1:50				3	18	23:10	M
	40	1:50				10	25	37:10	N
	50	1:40			3	21	37	63:10	O
	60	1:40			9	23	52	86:10	Z
	70	1:40			16	24	61	103:10	Z
FT.	80	1:30		3	19	35	72	131:10	Z
130	90	1:30		8	19	45	80	154:10	Z
42	10	–					0	2:20	*
M.	15	2:10					2	4:20	G
	20	2:10					6	8:20	I
	25	2:00				2	14	18:20	J
	30	2:00				5	21	28:20	K
	40	1:50			2	16	26	46:20	N
	50	1:50			6	24	44	76:20	O
	60	1:50			16	23	56	97:20	Z
FT.	70	1:40		4	19	32	68	125:20	Z
140	80	1:40		10	23	41	79	155:20	Z
45	5	–					0	2:30	C
M.	10	2:20					1	3:30	E
	15	2:20					3	5:30	G
	20	2:10				2	7	11:30	H
	25	2:10				4	17	23:30	K
	30	2:10				8	24	34.30	L
	40	2:00			5	19	33	59:30	N
	50	2:00			12	23	51	88:30	O
	60	1:50		3	19	26	62	112:30	Z
FT.	70	1:50		11	19	39	75	146:30	Z
150	80	1:40	1	17	19	50	84	173:30	Z
48	5	–					0	2:40	D
M.	10	2:30					1	3:40	F
	15	2:20				1	4	7:40	H
	20	2:20				3	11	16:40	J
	25	2:20				7	20	29:40	K
	30	2:10			2	11	25	40:40	M
	40	2:10			7	23	39	71:40	N
	50	2:00		2	16	23	55	98:40	Z
FT.	60	2:00		9	19	33	69	132:40	Z
160	70	1:50	1	17	22	44	80	166:40	Z
51	5	–					0	2:50	D
M.	10	2:40					2	4:50	F
	15	2:30				2	5	9:50	H
	20	2:30				4	15	21:50	J
	25	2:20			2	7	23	34:50	L
	30	2:20			4	13	26	45:50	M
	40	2:10		1	10	23	45	81:50	O
	50	2:10		5	18	23	61	109:50	Z
FT.	60	2:00	2	15	22	37	74	152:50	Z
170	70	2:00	8	17	19	51	86	183:50	Z
54	5	–					0	3:00	D
M.	10	2:50					3	6:00	F
	15	2:40				3	6	12:00	I
	20	2:30			1	5	17	26:00	K
	25	2:30			3	10	24	40:00	L
	30	2:30			6	17	27	53:00	N
	40	2:20		3	14	23	50	93:00	O
FT.	50	2:10	2	9	19	30	65	128:00	Z
180	60	2:10	5	16	19	44	81	168:00	Z
57	5	–					0	3:10	D
M.	10	2:50				1	3	7:10	G
	15	2:50				4	7	14:10	I
	20	2:40			2	6	20	31:10	K
	25	2:40			5	11	25	44:10	M
	30	2:30		1	8	19	32	63:10	N
	40	2:30		8	14	23	55	103:10	O
FT.	50	2:20	4	13	22	33	72	147:10	Z
190	60	2:20	10	17	19	50	84	183:10	Z

TABLE 1–12 SURFACE INTERVAL CREDIT TABLE

12:00 0:10	12:00 2:11	12:00 2:50	12:00 5:49	12:00 6:33	12:00 7:06	12:00 7:36	12:00 8:00	12:00 8:22	12:00 8:41	12:00 8:59	12:00 9:13	12:00 9:29	12:00 9:44	12:00 9:56	12:00 10:06
A	2:10 0:10	2:49 1:40	5:48 2:39	6:32 3:23	7:06 3:58	7:36 4:26	7:59 4:50	8:21 5:13	8:40 5:41	8:58 5:49	9:12 6:03	9:28 6:19	9:43 6:33	9:54 6:45	10:06 6:57
	B	1:39 0:10	2:38 1:10	3:22 1:58	3:57 2:29	4:25 2:59	4:49 3:21	5:12 3:44	5:40 4:03	5:48 4:20	6:02 4:36	6:18 4:50	6:32 5:04	6:44 5:17	6:56 5:28
		C	1:09 0:10	1:57 0:56	2:28 1:30	2:58 2:00	3:20 2:24	3:43 2:45	4:02 3:06	4:19 3:22	4:36 3:37	4:40 3:53	5:03 4:06	5:16 4:18	5:27 4:30
			D	0:54 0:10	1:29 0:46	1:59 1:16	2:23 1:42	2:44 2:03	3:04 2:21	3:21 2:39	3:36 2:54	3:52 3:09	4:04 3:23	4:17 3:34	4:29 3:46
				E	0:45 0:10	1:15 0:41	1:41 1:07	2:02 1:30	2:20 1:48	2:38 2:04	2:53 2:20	3:08 2:36	3:22 2:48	3:33 3:00	3:46 3:11
					F	0:40 0:10	1:06 0:37	1:29 1:00	1:47 1:20	2:03 1:36	2:19 1:50	2:34 2:06	2:47 2:19	2:59 2:30	3:10 2:43
						G	0:36 0:10	0:59 0:34	1:19 0:56	1:35 1:12	1:49 1:26	2:06 1:40	2:18 1:54	2:29 2:06	2:42 2:18
							H	0:33 0:10	0:54 0:32	1:11 0:50	1:26 1:05	1:39 1:19	1:53 1:31	2:04 1:44	2:17 1:56
								I	0:31 0:10	0:49 0:29	1:04 0:46	1:18 1:00	1:30 1:12	1:43 1:25	1:55 1:37
									J	0:28 0:10	0:46 0:27	0:59 0:43	1:11 0:56	1:24 1:08	1:36 1:19
										K	0:26 0:10	0:42 0:26	0:54 0:40	1:07 0:52	1:18 1:03
											L	0:25 0:10	0:39 0:25	0:51 0:37	1:02 0:49
												M	0:24 0:10	0:36 0:24	0:48 0:36
													N	0:23 0:10	0:34 0:23
														O	0:22 0:10
															Z

DEPTH mt.	DEPTH ft.	NO DECOMPRESSION LIMITS	REPETITIVE GROUPS														
			A	B	C	D	E	F	G	H	I	J	K	L	M	N	O
3	10	–	60	120	210	300											
4.5	15	–	35	70	110	160	225	350									
6	20	–	25	50	75	100	135	180	240	325							
7.5	25	–	20	35	55	75	100	125	160	195	245	315					
9	30	–	15	30	45	60	75	95	120	145	170	205	250	310			
10.5	35	310	5	15	25	40	50	60	80	100	120	140	160	190	220	270	310
12	40	200	5	15	25	30	40	50	70	80	100	110	130	150	170	200	
15	50	100	–	10	15	25	30	40	50	60	70	80	90	100			
18	60	60	–	10	15	20	25	30	40	50	55	60					
21	70	50	–	5	10	15	20	30	35	40	45	50					
24	80	40	–	5	10	15	20	25	30	35	40						
27	90	30	–	5	10	12	15	20	25	30							
30	100	25	–	5	7	10	15	20	22	25							
33	110	20	–	–	5	10	13	15	20								
36	120	15	–	–	5	10	12	15									
39	130	10	–	–	5	8	10										
42	140	10	–	–	5	7	10										
45	150	5	–	–	5												
48	160	5	–	–	–	5											
51	170	5	–	–	–	5											
54	180	5	–	–	–	5											
57	190	5	–	–	–	5											

TABLE 1–11 "NO DECOMPRESSION" LIMITS AND REPETITIVE GROUP DESIGNATION TABLE FOR "NO DECOMPRESSION" DIVES

CAUTION:

THESE "RESIDUAL NITROGEN TIMES" ARE THE TIMES A DIVER MUST ASSUME HE HAS *ALREADY SPENT* ON THE BOTTOM BEFORE HE *STARTS* A REPETITIVE DIVE TO A SPECIFIC DEPTH.

TABLE 1– 13

	REPETITIVE DIVE DEPTH															
ft.	40′	50′	60′	70′	80′	90′	100′	110′	120′	130′	140′	150′	160′	170′	180′	190′
mt.	12	15	18	21	24	27	30	33	36	39	42	45	48	51	54	57
A	7	6	5	4	4	3	3	3	3	3	2	2	2	2	2	2
B	17	13	11	9	8	7	7	6	6	6	5	5	4	4	4	4
C	25	21	17	15	13	11	10	10	9	8	7	7	6	6	6	6
D	37	29	24	20	18	16	14	13	12	11	10	9	9	8	8	8
E	49	38	30	26	23	20	18	16	15	13	12	12	11	10	10	10
F	61	47	36	31	28	24	22	20	18	16	15	14	13	13	12	11
G	73	56	44	37	32	29	26	24	21	19	18	17	16	15	14	13
H	87	66	52	43	38	33	30	27	25	22	20	19	18	17	16	15
I	101	76	61	50	43	38	34	31	28	25	23	22	20	19	18	17
J	116	87	70	57	48	43	38	34	32	28	26	24	23	22	20	19
K	138	99	79	64	54	47	43	38	35	31	29	27	26	24	22	21
L	161	111	88	72	61	53	48	42	39	35	32	30	28	26	25	24
M	187	124	97	80	68	58	52	47	43	38	35	32	31	29	27	26
N	213	142	107	87	73	64	57	51	46	40	38	35	33	31	29	28
O	241	160	117	96	80	70	62	55	50	44	40	38	36	34	31	30
Z	257	169	122	100	84	73	64	57	52	46	42	40	37	35	32	31

INSTRUCTIONS

ALL TABULATED BOTTOM TIMES (MINUTES), AND ALL TABULATED DEPTHS (FEET) HAVE BEEN TAKEN FROM THE U.S. NAVY DIVING MANUAL OF MARCH 1970.

TO CALCULATE A REPETITIVE DIVE UPON SURFACING FOR DIVES INVOLVING EXPOSURES UP TO AND INCLUDING THE "NO DECOMPRESSION LIMITS": ENTER TABLE 1-11 ON THE *EXACT* OR *NEXT GREATER DEPTH* THAN THAT TO WHICH EXPOSED, AND SELECT THE LISTED EXPOSURE TIME *EXACT* OR *NEXT GREATER* THAN THE ACTUAL EXPOSURE TIME. THE REPETITIVE GROUP DESIGNATION IS INDICATED BY THE LETTER AT THE HEAD OF THE VERTICAL COLUMN WHERE THE SELECTED EXPOSURE TIME IS LISTED.

CONTINUE THE VERTICAL MOTION ALONG THE STRAIGHT LINES JOINING TABLE 1-11 TO TABLE 1-12. ENTER THE TABLE *VERTICALLY* TO SELECT THE ELAPSED SURFACE INTERVAL TIME. THE NEW REPETITIVE GROUP DESIGNATION FOR THE SURFACE INTERVAL IS TO THE RIGHT OF THE HORIZONTAL COLUMN WHERE THE ELAPSED SURFACE INTERVAL TIME IS LISTED.

CONTINUE THE RIGHTHANDED MOTION TO ENTER 1-13 ON THE HORIZONTAL COLUMN TO THE RIGHT OF THE NEW REPETITIVE GROUP DESIGNATION. THE TIME IN EACH VERTICAL COLUMN IS THE RESIDUAL NITROGEN TIME. IT IS A PENALTY TIME; ie, THE TIME A DIVER MUST ASSUME HE HAS *ALREADY SPENT* ON THE BOTTOM *BEFORE HE STARTS* A REPETITIVE DIVE TO THE DEPTH SPECIFIED AT THE BOTTOM OF THE COLUMN.

APPENDIX No. 6
BEAUFORT WIND SCALE

BEAUFORT WIND SCALE

Beaufort International Number	Wind	Max. Speed kts.	Max. Speed m.p.h.	Sea Indications	Land Indications
0	Calm	< 1	< 1	Sea mirror smooth	Smoke rises vertically.
1	Light air	3	3	Small wavelets like scales, no foam crests	Direction shown by smoke but not by wind vanes.
2	Light breeze	6	7	Waves short and more pronounced; crests begin to break; foam has glassy appearance – not yet white	Wind felt on face; leaves rustle, ordinary vanes moved by wind.
3	Gentle breeze	10	12		Leaves and small twigs in constant motion; wind extends light flag.
4	Moderate breeze	16	18	Waves are longer; many white horses	Raises dust and waste paper; small branches are moved.
5	Fresh breeze	21	24	Waves now pronounced and long; white foam crests everywhere	Small trees in leaf begin to sway; crested wavelets form on inland waters.
6	Strong breeze	27	31	Larger waves form; white foam crests more extensive	Large branches in motion; whistling heard in telegraph wires; umbrellas used with difficulty.
7	Strong wind*	33	38	Sea heaps up; wind starts to blow the foam in streaks	Whole trees in motion; inconvenience felt when walking against wind.
8	Fresh gale	40	46	Height of waves increases visibly also height of crests; much foam is blown in dense streaks	Breaks twigs off trees; greatly impedes progress.
9	Strong gale	47	54		Slight structural damage occurs (chimney pots and slates removed).
10	Whole gale	55	63	High waves with long overhanging crests great foam patches	Seldom experienced inland; trees uprooted; considerable structural damage occurs.
11	Storm	65	75	Waves so high that ships within sight are hidden in the throughs; sea covered with streaky foam; air filled with spray	Very rarely experienced; accompanied by widespread damage.
12	Hurricane	above 65	above 75		–

*On land, force 7 is designated as "moderate gale".

Other publications from SEAPEN BOOKS
Written and designed by Shlomo Cohen

Bahamas Diver's Guide

A uniqe guidebook in sport-diving media. 184 pages in full color printed on fine chrome paper, describing the best diving sites in the Bahamas. The descriptions of the sites include landmarks and sea bearings with accompanying photos, latitudes and longitudes for sea charts. Aerial photographs of the sites with transparent overleaf pointing out salient features, underwater photos, locations, etc. The Fish Index provides 65 of the most common species found by divers in Bahamien waters. Special Medicine chapter and a Comfort Index.

The Sea I Love
An outstandingly designed Album, 24,5x23 cm (9,5″x9″), describing the underwater world of the Red Sea, with photographs, illustrations and text. 94 pages, printed in full color on fine chrome paper.

Red Sea Underwater Fish-Guide

You can share the unique underwater world of the Red Sea with your family by snorkeling with this full-color waterproof book. It provides 65 of the most common species in the Red Sea. Identified by color photographs captioned with both their common and scientific names, plus a brief text identifying them and indicating where they can be found. Printed on waterproof plastic paper with rust-proof binding.

THE SCHOOL OF U/W PHOTOGRAPHY EILAT ISRAEL

DIVE INTO A NEW DIMENSION

UNDERWATER PHOTOGRAPHY IN EILAT AND THE RED SEA

*Add a new dimension to the marvels of Eilat and the Red Sea experience the world of **underwater photography and video** through a series of beginner and advanced courses and seminars conducted by internationally famous underwater photographer David Pilosof at the **School of Underwater Photography, Eilat.***

Courses include:

* *Discovering Underwater Photography - half-day introductory course (camera provided).*
* *Introduction to Underwater Video - half-day course (video equipment provided).*
* *Open Water Photography - 5 day course, day and night dives, development and analysis.*
* *Video Down Under - 5 day course in basic underwater video production.*
* *The Samantha Experience - 5 day advanced seminar, including photography of models.*

NEW - THE LITTLE PHOTO SHOP!

*Operated by the **School of Underwater Photography** on King Solomon's Wharf, Eilat. This "big little shop" offers:*

* *Quick film processing.*
* *Film, batteries, Red Sea Video cassettes.*
* ***Underwater photo equipment:** sale, rental and **DUTY-FREE PURCHASE.***

The School of Underwater Photography - The Little Photo Shop
King Solomon's Wharf, North Beach, Eilat 88000, Israel.
Tel: (059) 79628. Telex: 341667 IL Att. D.P./966. Fax: (03) 236926
Att. D.P./966.

FANTASEA Cruises

RED SEA DIVERS - FANTASEA

We're back, and better than ever!
Welcome to the world of Red Sea diving. Of all the enchanting places to spend a diving holiday, none surpass the Red Sea!
We should know! We established our first diving operation here in 1971, and for over a decade pioneered diving tourism to the area. Over 20,000 divers have shared the holiday of a lifetime with us!

Join us for a cruise aboard the premier diving yacht in the Red Sea. Bi-weekly departures from Eilat for 7 - 10 day diving adventures to the reefs of Ras Mohammed, the Straits of Tiran, the Dunraven Shipwreck and many more.

Price includes 3 dives daily, guide, tanks, refills and weights. Guests stay in comfortable, air-conditioned accommodation and enjoy the excellent cuisine prepared by our professional crew.

Special group rates available.

Over 15 years of experience in quality diving services in the Red Sea.

For reservations and further information contact: Howard Rosenstein
P.O. Box 420, Herzliya Bet, Israel 46130. Tel: (053) 666482.
Telex: 35770 COIN IL, Attn: DIVERS.